A Handful of Herbs

KAY FRANCIS
WITH PAMELA ALLARDICE

PHOTOGRAPHY BY ROWAN FOTHERINGHAM

BayBooks

An imprint of HarperCollins*Publishers*

Contents

SAGE FLOWERS

CHIVE AND FENNEL FLOWERS

Introduction

Many of the popular herbs are easy to grow, if given the right conditions, but it is recognized that not all cooks have gardens.

Most of the herbs used in the recipes in this book can generally be found in supermarkets and vegetable markets (these herbs are indicated by an asterisk*). Other herbs are more readily available from specialty vegetable markets or Asian grocers (these herbs are indicated by two asterisks**).

BASIL* (*Ocimum* species) is in great demand, usually sweet green basil (*O. basilicum*) or one of its varieties with smaller leaves, such as 'bush basil' (*O. basilicum* 'Minimum') and lemon basil (*O. basilicum* 'Citriodora'). Opal basil (*O. basilicum* 'Purpurascens'), also called purple basil, is now more readily available, particularly in larger cities.

BAY LEAVES* are leaves from the sweet bay tree (*Laurus nobilis*), also known as roman laurel. Although it is not strictly a herb, the leaves are commonly used for flavouring food, and they are one of the ingredients of bouquet garni. Dried leaves are readily available from supermarkets.

CHERVIL** (*Anthriscus cerefolium*) is not sold in great quantities because its flavour doesn't last long after harvesting, nor is it as easy as other herbs for growers to maintain. It is one of the ingredients in fines herbes.

CHILLI* (*Capsicum* species), also known as hot pepper and chili pepper, is available in many varieties, ranging from the mild banana chilli to the very hot birdseye. There is a trend towards the exotic yellow, orange and brown chilli varieties.

CHIVES* are available in two varieties: those with hollow tubular stems and mauve flowers, called common chives or grass onions (*Allium schoenoprasum*), and those with flat leaves and white flowers, called garlic chives or Chinese chives (*A. tuberosum*). Chive flowers are edible, and can sometime be found in vegetable markets. Chives are one of the ingredients in fines herbes.

CORIANDER* (*Coriandrum sativum*), also known as Chinese parsley, cilantro, and Indian parsley, has become increasingly popular since the late 1970s with the increased interest in Thai, Vietnamese and Asian foods. Fresh coriander is readily available. Chopped, bottled coriander is available in some supermarkets.

CRESS* is generally sold in sprout form rather than in bunches. Watercress (*Nasturtium officinale*) and land cress (*Lepidum sativum*) are big sellers in supermarkets.

DILL* (*Anethum graveolens*) can be found in small quantities in markets or speciality shops, particularly in summer.

FENNEL* is available as a bulb vegetable (*Foeniculum vulgare* var. *azoricum*), commonly called aniseed, and as a leaf (*Foeniculum vulgare*). Bronze fennel (*Foeniculum vulgare* var. *rubrum*) is now making its appearance as a gourmet herb.

GARLIC* (*Allium sativum*) is sold in enormous quantities, as a fresh bulb or processed into bottles or paste. Despite its being an extremely popular herb, it is not often grown in herb gardens, because it can be difficult.

GINGER* (*Zingiber officinale*) is one of the most popular spices and is easily obtainable, both fresh and processed.

HORSERADISH* (*Amoracia rusticana*) is a perennial herb, the root of which is grated to make sauce. Horseradish is sometimes grown in herb gardens, but few gardeners bother to harvest it for use in the kitchen as much of what is grown is very fibrous and tough. Bottles of grated horseradish are available from supermarkets.

LEMON BALM** (*Melissa officinalis*) is sold mainly for use as a herbal tea. Generally found in mixed bunches.

LEMON GRASS* (*Cymbopogon citratus*) is a popular herb in Thai cooking, and is quite readily available. The lower, paler part of the leaf is available in a preserved form, in bottles, from supermarkets.

LOVAGE** (*Levistum officinalis*) is powerfully aromatic, and is used sparingly. Often grown in herb gardens.

MARJORAM* (*Origanum majorana*), also known as sweet marjoram, is occasionally called oregano (*Origanum vulgare*). Sweet marjoram has a sweet spicy aroma and flavour, unlike oregano.

MINT* is available through most outlets. The most readily available is common garden mint (*Mentha spicata*), which is sometimes called spearmint (true spearmint has a distinct spearmint-toothpaste flavour). Peppermint (*Mentha x piperita*), apple mint (*Mentha suaveolens*), and pineapple mint (*Mentha suaveolens* 'Variegata') are also available.

NASTURTIUM (*Trapaeolum majus*), also called Indian cress, is a herb commonly grown in gardens but rarely found in vegetable markets. The leaves, flowers and seeds are edible.

OREGANO* (*Origanum vulgare*) is occasionally called wild marjoram (not to be confused with sweet marjoram (*Origamum majorana*). Oregano has a pungent peppery aroma and flavour, and is often used in Italian, Mexican and Spanish cooking. Some golden oregano is to be found, but it is mainly used as a garnish.

PARSLEY* is the herb most commonly sold, especially the curly parsley (*Petroselinum crispum*). The flat-leaf Italian or Continental parsley (*Petroselinum neopolitanum*) has a stronger flavour and is often used in middle-eastern cookery. Most parsley sold isn't eaten, however, but merely pushed around a plate before being thrown out, proving a terrific market for the growers! Parsley is used in bouquet garni and fines herbes.

PERILLA** (*Perilla frutescens*) is a fragrant, fruity Japanese herb with overtones of mint. It is available in small amounts from some specialty grocers, particularly where there is a large Japanese population. Purple perilla (aka-jiso), sometimes called 'beefsteak plant', is more common than green, and is added to sashimi, confectionery and pickles such as umeboshi. Fresh leaves of green perilla (ao-jiso) are often added to rolled sushi; they are also used as a garnish, or fried in tempura batter.

ROSEMARY* (*Rosmarinus officinalis*) is a popular herb, commonly grown in many gardens and harvested all year round. It is found in some markets and greengrocers.

SAGE* (*Salvia officinalis*) has tended to be associated with run-of-the-mill foods of British origin and hasn't the appeal of herbs associated with more exotic foods. Sage is one herb that needs a facelift: try deep-fried sage leaves and sage and walnut pesto! Apart from the main variety, which has grey-green leaves, there is also red or purple sage (*Salvia officinalis purpurea*), and the delicious pineapple-flavoured form (*Salvia rutans*).

SALAD BURNET** (*Poterium sanguisorba*) has a slight cucumber flavour, and is very attractive as a garnish. Young leaves are delicious in salads.

SAVORY** usually refers to winter savory (*Satureja montana*), which is the perennial. It has a very aromatic resinous flavour, and is especially used to flavour beans, hot pots, and casseroles. Summer savory (*Satureja hortensis*) is an annual, and is sweeter than winter savory. Savory is usually sold in mixed bunches.

SORREL* is the name by which both French sorrel (*Rumex scutatus*) and garden sorrel (*Rumex acetosa*) are known. French sorrel is regarded as being more succulent than garden sorrel. Sorrel is easily grown, so one doesn't always see it for sale except in very large markets.

SUMMER SAVORY—see Savory

TARRAGON* in cookery refers to French (or 'true') tarragon (*Artemisia dracunculus*), and is mainly found in gourmet or specialty shops. It is one of the ingredients of fines herbes, and is used to flavour vinegar. Russian tarragon (*Artemesia dracunculoides*), also called 'false' tarragon, has far less flavour. Try before you buy!

THYME* (*Thymus vulgaris*) is usually available from greengrocers. Lemon thyme (*Thymus x citriodorus*) is also sold, as is caraway-scented thyme (*Thymus herbabarona*), but not in great quantities. Thyme is one of the ingredients of bouquet garni.

VIETNAMESE MINT* (*Polygonum odoratum*) and coriander are among the most popular 'exotic' herbs sought by anyone with an interest in eastern foods. Available from outlets offering a range of unusual vegetables and herbs. The flavour can vary, depending on the quality of the plant, so try before you buy (if possible) or buy from a shop patronized by the Asian population.

WATERCRESS—see Cress

Occasionally in vegetable markets you will also find other herbs, such as **CURRY TREE LEAF**, **CURRY PLANT** and **BERGAMOT**.

Japanese 'herbs' such as **MIZUMA**, **KOMATSUMA** and **MIBUNA** are available through major markets but these are classified as vegetables rather than herbs.

Herb flowers such as **BORAGE**, **BERGAMOT**, **VIOLETS**, **JOHNNY JUMP-UPS** and **CALENDULA** are more readily available now but they are usually included in mesclun (mixed salad greens) rather than being sold on their own.

CORIANDER

CHERVIL

TARRAGON

OPAL BASIL

MINT

THYME

LEMON GRASS

LEMON BALM

OREGANO

FENNEL

BASIL

VIETNAMESE
MINT

SAGE

LOVAGE

ROSEMARY

CHIVES AND
CHIVE FLOWERS

BORAGE AND
BORAGE FLOWERS

SORREL

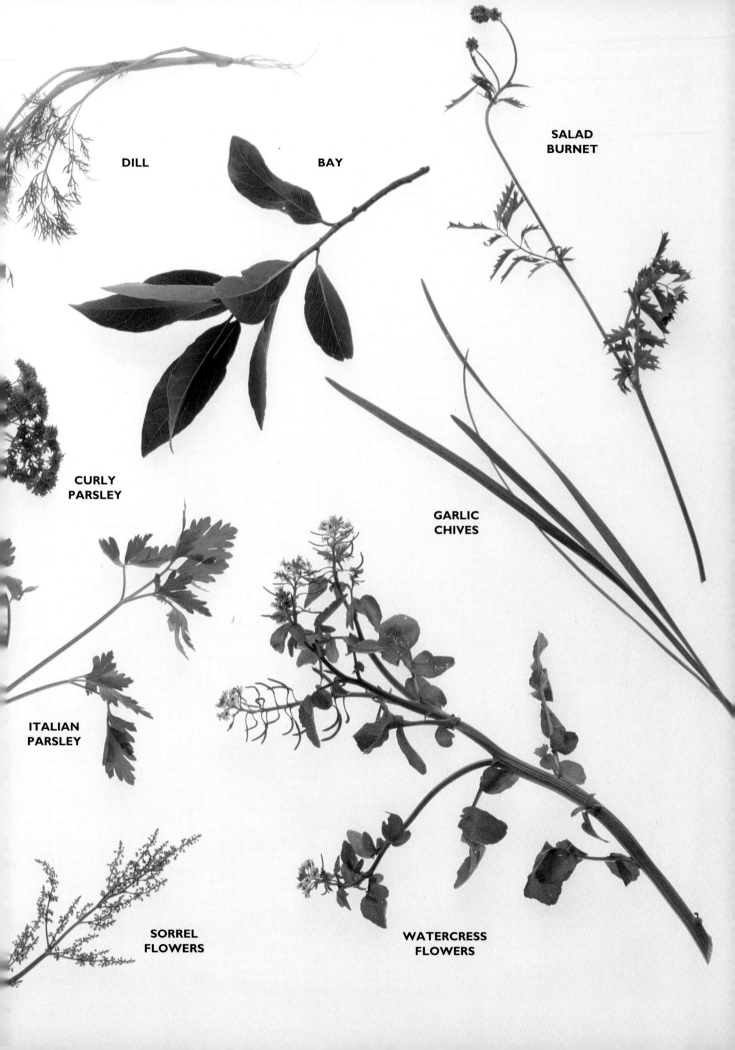

DILL

BAY

SALAD
BURNET

CURLY
PARSLEY

GARLIC
CHIVES

ITALIAN
PARSLEY

SORREL
FLOWERS

WATERCRESS
FLOWERS

Soups, Snacks and Starters

Chicken Stock

Vegetable Stock

Beef Stock

Sour Prawn and Scallop Soup

Carrot Soup with Chervil Cream

Jerusalem Artichoke Soup

Pumpkin Soup with Dill

Icy Yoghurt Mint Drink

Fresh Tomato Soup

Prawn Pouches with Dipping Sauce

Basil Tea

Capsicum and Mozzarella Tortilla Bites

Herbed Cheese Tartlets

Deep-fried Sage Leaves

Bocconcini Preserved in Olive Oil

**Bruschetta with Grilled Eggplant
and Preserved Bocconcini**

Stuffed Nasturtium Leaves

Dill-marinated Ocean Trout

BRUSCHETTA WITH GRILLED EGGPLANT AND PRESERVED BOCCONCINI,
PAGE 26 (Photographed at Milkwood. Christopher Vine platter from Plumes Gift
Agencies. Emile Henry yellow bowl from The Bay Tree. Pillivuyt plates from Hale
Imports)

In this book, when we speak of GREEN ONIONS, we are referring to young spring onions, which have small slender pale green bulbs, mid green stems, and long dark green hollow leaves. These are (confusingly) called GREEN SHALLOTS in some parts of Australia, and SCALLIONS or SPRING ONIONS in other parts of the English-speaking world. They are sold in bunches, and have a fresh onion flavour.

When we speak of SPRING ONIONS, we are referring to the mature spring onion, with a white bulb and long hollow leaves. Spring onions are sold in bunches, and have a mild onion flavour.

When we speak of GOLDEN SHALLOTS we are referring to the tear-drop shaped golden-brown bulbs with papery skins, similar in appearance to but considerably larger than garlic. GOLDEN SHALLOTS are also known as TRUE FRENCH SHALLOTS, ESCHALOTS and GOLDEN ONIONS. They have a subtle but pervasive onion flavour.

CHICKEN STOCK

MAKES ABOUT 6 CUPS (1.5 LITRES/48 FL OZ)

For Asian recipes, instead of the bay leaf, use 1 fresh or dried kaffir lime leaf and 1 stalk fresh lemon grass.

- **1 kg (2 lb) chicken bones and giblets**
- **1 stick celery**
- **1 onion, quartered**
- **1 carrot, chopped**
- **10 black peppercorns**
- **1 bay leaf**

Combine ingredients in a large pot, and cover with cold water. Slowly bring to the boil, skimming occasionally. Simmer, partially covered, for 2 to 3 hours.

Strain through a muslin-lined sieve.

Refrigerate the stock until the fat has solidified on the surface.

Remove the fat, strain stock into a clean saucepan and use in a recipe, or strain into a storage container and refrigerate or freeze until required.

VEGETABLE STOCK

MAKES ABOUT 4 CUPS (1 LITRE/32 FL OZ)

- **2 carrots, quartered**
- **1 unpeeled onion, quartered**
- **1 stick celery, plus a few leafy tops**
- **1 bay leaf**
- **2 sprigs parsley**
- **1 sprig rosemary**
- **8 black peppercorns**
- **1 teaspoon salt**

Combine ingredients in a large pot and cover with cold water. Simmer gently for 40 to 50 minutes. Strain, and store until required.

BEEF STOCK

MAKES ABOUT 2 LITRES (64 FL OZ)

- **1 kg (2 lb) beef marrow bones, sawn into pieces**
- **1 tablespoon mustard seeds**
- **1 tablespoon black peppercorns**
- **2 brown onions, unpeeled, and quartered**
- **1 stick celery**
- **2 carrots, halved**
- **½ head fennel**
- **2 fresh bay leaves**
- **few sprigs parsley**
- **few sprigs chervil**
- **few sprigs thyme**
- **1 small knob freshly dug garlic or 2 to 3 unpeeled, crushed cloves**

Place bones in a large stockpot, and cover. Cook over a high heat, turning occasionally, until brown.

Add mustard seeds and peppercorns, cover, and cook over a high heat until mustard seeds begin to pop.

Add remaining ingredients and cold water to within 7.5 cm (3 in) from the top of the pot. Reduce temperature to lowest heat, partially cover pot and leave to simmer gently for 6 to 8 hours. Skim surface occasionally.

Strain contents of pan through a muslin- or disposable cloth-lined sieve. Discard solids and return liquid to a clean pot.

Boil for 1 hour to reduce liquid, skimming frequently.

Cool, and skim off any solids which set on the surface. Strain again through a lined sieve.

Refrigerate until required, or decant into smaller containers and freeze.

SOUR PRAWN AND SCALLOP SOUP, PAGE 16
(Soup spoon from The Bay Tree)

BAY

Bay leaves and bay branches tossed onto a barbecue fire will add flavour to cooking meat.

SOUR PRAWN AND SCALLOP SOUP

SERVES 6

6 cups (1.5 litres/48 fl oz) home-made chicken stock (recipe, page 14)

3 stalks fresh lemon grass, sliced

2 kaffir lime leaves (fresh or dried)

3 slices fresh ginger root

½ cup (125 ml/4 fl oz) lime juice

3 fresh red chillies (chili peppers), seeded and sliced

500 g (1 lb) green king prawns (shrimps), peeled to the tail and deveined

500 g (1 lb) scallops

150 g (5 oz) fresh black cloud-ear mushrooms (see note)

150 g (5 oz) fresh white fungi or golden mushrooms (see note)

2 tablespoons chopped fresh coriander leaves and stalks

2 green onions (green shallots or scallions), sliced

2 tablespoons fish sauce (see note)

Place stock, lemon grass, lime leaves, ginger, lime juice and chillies in a saucepan. Bring to the boil, and simmer for 10 minutes.

Stand the saucepan off the heat for 10 minutes, then strain the mixture through a muslin-lined sieve into a clean saucepan.

Bring to the boil, add prawns, scallops, and mushrooms, and cook until prawns change colour, about 2 minutes.

Add remaining ingredients, and serve immediately.

Notes: Black cloud-ear mushrooms, white fungi and golden mushrooms are available from stores specialising

---

CORIANDER

Coriander is an annual herb with highly aromatic leaves and seeds. It is a very ancient herb, originating in southern Europe and the Middle East. The Greek physician Hippocrates (460-377 BC) prescribed it as a digestive aid. Greek and Roman physicians are thought to have popularized coriander amongst the Egyptians, both as a medicine and as a food preservative. It is mentioned in the Old Testament as one of the 'bitter herbs' eaten at Passover. The Bible also refers to manna, which God fed to the Children of Israel when they were starving in the wilderness, as tasting of coriander seeds.

---

in Asian vegetables. You can, however, substitute 1 can (425 g/14 oz) straw mushrooms, drained.

Fish sauce is readily available from Asian supermarkets; it is generally called *nam pla* (Thai fish sauce) or *nuoc mam* (Vietnamese fish sauce).

CARROT SOUP WITH CHERVIL CREAM

SERVES 6 TO 8

60 g (2 oz) butter

4 large golden shallots (French shallots or eschalots), finely chopped

1 kg (2 lb) young carrots, peeled and diced

---

8 cups (2 litres/64 fl oz) chicken stock (recipe, page 14)

½ teaspoon cumin seeds

1 teaspoon salt

1 teaspoon freshly ground black pepper

½ cup (125 ml/4 fl oz) sour cream

3 tablespoons chopped chervil, and extra for garnish

Melt butter in a large, heavy based saucepan over low heat. Add shallots, cover, and cook for 10 minutes, or until shallots are soft.

Add carrots and stir well. Cover pot, and cook over low heat for 10 minutes, stirring occasionally.

Add stock, cumin, and salt and pepper. Cook, partly covered, over a medium heat for 30 minutes, or until carrots are tender.

Purée in the saucepan by using a hand-held food processor, or transfer to a blender, blend until smooth and return soup to the saucepan. Taste for seasonings. Reheat.

Serve in individual bowls. Garnish with sour cream and chervil.

CHERVIL

The botanical name for chervil, *Choerphyllum*, is derived from the Greek for 'warms the heart', a reference to its 'warming' aniseed-like fragrance. It is thought to have been one of the 'warming spices' that Moses used to prepare the holy oil to consecrate the Tabernacle.

JERUSALEM ARTICHOKE SOUP

SERVES 4

60 g (2 oz) butter

2 leeks, washed and sliced

500 g (1 lb) Jerusalem artichokes, washed and sliced

1 tablespoon lemon thyme leaves

2 cups (500 ml/16 fl oz) chicken stock (recipe, page 14)

2 cups (500 ml/16 fl oz) milk

½ cup (125 ml/4 fl oz) sour cream

3 tablespoons finely snipped chives

2 tablespoons finely grated lemon rind

salt and freshly ground black pepper

Melt butter in a large, deep saucepan and add leek and artichokes. Cover, and cook over a low heat for 20 minutes, stirring occasionally.

Add lemon thyme, chicken stock, milk, and salt and pepper to taste; increase heat and bring to a simmer. Reduce heat, partially cover, and simmer for 30 minutes.

Blend by using a hand-held food processor in the saucepan, or transfer the soup to a blender and process until smooth.

Reheat, then serve garnished with sour cream, chives, lemon rind, and freshly ground black pepper.

PUMPKIN SOUP WITH DILL

SERVES 6 TO 8

This soup is especially good when accompanied by warm focaccia.

1 kg (2 lb) ham bones

30 g (1 oz) butter

1 large onion, chopped

1 kg (2 lb) peeled and seeded pumpkin, cut into large dice

2 tablespoons snipped dill leaves, and extra for garnish

1 teaspoon salt

1 teaspoon freshly ground black pepper

Place ham bones in a large pot, cover, and cook gently for 10 minutes, stirring occasionally.

Add butter and onion, cover, and cook 10 minutes more.

Add pumpkin, and water to cover, then add dill, salt and pepper. Cover pot, and simmer gently over low heat for 45 to 60 minutes.

Remove bones. Blend soup in the pot with a hand-held food processor, or transfer soup to a blender and process until smooth.

Remove meat from bones, cut into chunks and return to pot. Check seasonings. Reheat soup.

Serve sprinkled with extra dill.

ICY YOGHURT MINT DRINK

SERVES 6

- **2 cups (500 ml/16 fl oz) buttermilk**
- **2 cups (500 ml/16 fl oz) plain yoghurt**
- **¼ teaspoon salt**
- **70 g (2¼ oz) sugar**
- **1 teaspoon fresh ginger juice (see note)**
- **2 teaspoons lemon juice**
- **½ cup mint leaves, slightly crushed**

Blend together all ingredients except mint, until sugar is fully dissolved.

Pour into a large jug, and stir in mint. Chill thoroughly.

To serve, strain over ice cubes in tall glasses.

Note: To obtain the juice from fresh ginger, grate a 5 cm (2 in) piece of peeled ginger root into a cup lined with a piece of disposable kitchen cloth or muslin. Twist the cloth into a pouch and squeeze the juice from the ginger into the cup.

ICY YOGHURT MINT DRINK
(La Rochere jug and glasses from Studio Haus. Napkins from Les Olivades. 'Wave' table and chair from Potter Williams)

MINT

Mint came originally from the Mediterranean region. The Greeks and Romans crowned themselves with mint for banquets, and put bunches on the table in the hope of warding off drunkenness. The Romans also rubbed mint leaves over banquet tables to stir up ' a greedy taste for meate'. Ending a meal with a sprig of mint to help the digestion and sweeten the breath is a very ancient custom, culminating in the widespread popularity of 'after dinner' mints, still used today.

Mint tea has been used for many centuries in different cultures, and has a pronounced cooling effect—add it to fruit punches and salads in summertime. Even just mixing a pinch of dried mint with a brew of regular tea makes for a refreshing change. Apple mint gives an interesting zing to summer fruit salads, puddings and other cold desserts. A superb vinegar can be made from pineapple mint.

FRESH TOMATO SOUP

SERVES 4

60 g (2 oz) butter

1 medium bulb fennel, chopped

4 golden shallots (French shallots or eschalots)

1 clove garlic, finely chopped

750 g (1½ lb) vine-ripened tomatoes, peeled and chopped

1 cup (250 ml/8 fl oz) chicken stock (recipe, page 14)

1 bay leaf

4 sprigs fresh thyme, and extra for garnish

1 thinly pared strip orange rind

salt and freshly ground black pepper

½ cup crème fraîche

Melt butter in a deep pan. Add fennel, shallots and garlic, and stir over a medium heat until vegetables have softened. Add remaining ingredients, except crème fraîche and cook slowly, covered, for 30 minutes.

Remove bay leaf and thyme, then purée contents of pan using a hand-held food processor or blender.

Add salt and pepper to taste.

Reheat and serve, garnished with crème fraîche and sprinkled with thyme leaves.

FENNEL

'The fennel seed is much used in pippen pies and diveres other baked fruits, as also into bread to give it more relish.'

—John Parkinson, 1629

PRAWN POUCHES WITH DIPPING SAUCE

MAKES 25

25 sheets filo (phyllo)

25 thin strips lemon grass (blanched) or chives, for tying pouches

3 cups (750 ml/24 fl oz) peanut oil, for deep-frying

FILLING

1 large carrot, peeled and grated

100 g (3 oz) bean sprouts

100 g (3 oz) fresh black cloud-ear mushrooms, finely sliced (see note)

6 spring onions, finely chopped

½ cup Vietnamese mint, chopped

4 cloves garlic, crushed

2.5 cm (1 in) fresh ginger root, grated

250 g (8 oz) green prawns (shrimps), peeled, deveined and roughly chopped

SAUCE

1½ tablespoons raw sugar

4 cloves garlic, crushed

2 small red chillies (chili peppers), finely sliced

½ cup (125 ml/4 fl oz) lime juice

½ cup (125 ml/4 fl oz) fish sauce (see note, page 16)

Fold each filo sheet in half.

Combine the ingredients for the filling. Spoon the mixture into the centre of the folded filo, leaving enough free edge to pull up and form the pouch. Tie with lemon grass or chives and leave on a wire rack to dry.

Combine the ingredients for the sauce.

Just before serving, heat oil in a deep pan, add the dried pouches in small batches and fry until just golden. Drain on absorbent paper.

Serve hot, with the dipping sauce in a separate bowl.

Note: Vietnamese mint and fresh black cloud-ear mushrooms are available from stores specialising in Asian vegetables. If you cannot obtain fresh mushrooms, substitute dried black cloud-ear mushrooms (soak in warm water for 30 minutes, drain and slice).

VIETNAMESE MINT

Vietnamese mint, despite its name, is not really a member of the mint family. Rather than the cooling taste of mint, Vietnamese mint is very hot indeed. It is native to Indochina, being much used in Vietnamese cookery as well as in the cuisine of Thailand and other Asian countries. Use the fresh young leaves to add a hot spicy flavour to a recipe; it is especially delicious with chicken. Or shred it and add it to salads, or simply use as a garnish. Use it sparingly at first until you get used to its peppery taste and strong pungent flavour.

BASIL TEA

SERVES 2

½ cup basil leaves

2 cups (500 ml/16 fl oz) water

2 teaspoons or 2 teabags orange
   pekoe tea

1 thin slice fresh ginger root

1 tablespoon honey, or to taste

milk, optional

Combine basil and water in a small
pan. Bring to boil, then cover
pan. Reduce heat and brew for
5 minutes.

Add tea, ginger and honey. Stir well
and bring to a boil. Remove from
heat, stand for 3 minutes, and strain
into tea cups.

If milk is desired, add it after
pouring the tea.

BASIL

Basil is best known as a
culinary herb. Early English
manuscripts record its use in
'sallets' and 'green pottages'
along with all manner of
pickles. A true 'herb of the
sun', basil will enhance the
flavour of all summer
vegetables, especially tomatoes,
and will add zest to savoury
dishes, pâtés, stuffings, sauces
and soups. The Italians pound
fresh basil into their famous
pesto sauce, along with garlic
and Parmesan cheese.

MARJORAM

Marjoram has been a popular
sweet herb since ancient times.
It has a subtle and warming
flavour and aroma, and is
delicious with sausages and
meat dishes, vegetarian and
bean or nut dishes, salads,
omelettes, herb scones, in
sauces and in vinegars. It goes
particularly well with pasta, in
pizza, and with tomatoes. If you
are using fresh marjoram, use
only the leaves and flower
tops, not the stems.

CAPSICUM AND MOZZARELLA TORTILLA BITES

MAKES 32

8 soft flour tortillas (each 20 cm/
   8 in)

1 medium Spanish onion, finely
   chopped

1 red or yellow capsicum (sweet
   pepper), roasted, peeled and
   cut into strips (see note)

250 g (8 oz) mozzarella cheese,
   grated

2 cloves garlic, finely chopped

2 tablespoons chopped fresh
   marjoram

2 tablespoons chopped fresh
   oregano

freshly ground black pepper

2 tablespoons oil

paprika, for dusting

Preheat oven to 200°C (400°F).

Soften the tortillas by heating in a
heavy frying pan for 30 seconds on
each side.

Combine onion, capsicum, cheese,
garlic and herbs, and spread down
the centre third of each tortilla. Roll
tortillas from one edge to form a
tube enclosing the filling. Brush
with oil.

Place rolls on oven trays and bake
for 15 minutes, or until cheese is
melted and tortillas are golden.

Sprinkle with paprika, cut
diagonally into 5 cm (2 in) lengths,
and serve.

Note: To roast capsicum, halve,
remove seeds and place cut-side
down under a hot grill until the
skin blackens; or place capsicum in
a hot oven and roast for about
20 minutes, or until the clear skin
begins to blister. In both cases,
place blackened or blistered
capsicum into a bowl, cover, and
leave for 10 minutes. Peel. (Juices
that accumulate in the bowl can be
used in the recipe or reserved to
flavour another dish.)

MARJORAM

To make marjoram conserve:
'Take the tops and tenderest
parts of Sweet Marjoram,
bruise it well in a wooden
Mortar or Bowl; take double
the weight of Fine Sugar, boil it
with Marjoram Water till it is
as thick as Syrup, then put in
your beaten Marjoram.'

—*The Receipts of John Nott,
Cook to the Duke of Bolton,*
1723

HERBED CHEESE TARTLETS

MAKES 12

PASTRY

- 250 g (8 oz) unbleached bread flour
- 2 tablespoons sesame seeds, toasted (see note)
- pinch of salt
- ½ teaspoon paprika
- 125 g (4 oz) butter, and extra for greasing patty tins
- 2 tablespoons lemon juice
- iced water to mix (about 5 tablespoons)

FILLING

- 250 g (8 oz) farmer's cheese (see note)
- 1 tablespoon chopped chervil, and extra for garnish
- 1 tablespoon chopped tarragon
- 1 teaspoon snipped chives
- 3 tablespoons thick cream
- 12 black olives, stoned and sliced
- salt and freshly ground black pepper

TO MAKE THE PASTRY

Combine flour, sesame seeds and paprika with a pinch of salt. Rub in the butter until mixture resembles fine breadcrumbs.

Stir in the lemon juice and enough water to form a soft dough.

Form the dough into a disc, wrap it in plastic, and chill for 15 minutes.

Preheat oven to 200°C (400°F). Grease 12 patty tins.

Roll dough out on a floured surface, and line the greased patty tins with it. Prick the base of each pastry case.

Refrigerate for 15 minutes.

Bake pastry cases for 15 minutes, or until crisp and golden. While cases are cooking, make the filling.

TO MAKE THE FILLING

Beat together cheese, herbs and cream until smooth. Stir in olives and seasonings.

Spoon filling into the cases, garnish each tart with a small sprig of chervil, grind black pepper over, and serve immediately.

Notes: To toast the sesame seeds, place in microwave for 2 minutes or in hot oven (200°C/400°F) for 5 minutes.

Farmer's cheese is a firm cottage cheese.

HERBED CHEESE TARTLETS
(Photographed at Milkwood. Christopher Vine platter from Plumes Gift Agencies)

DEEP-FRIED SAGE LEAVES

MAKES 25

Tasty nibbles to accompany drinks.

25 fresh sage leaves, washed and dried

3 cups (750 ml/24 fl oz) light olive oil

sea salt, to serve

2 limes, cut into wedges

BATTER

120 g (4 oz) unbleached plain flour

¼ teaspoon salt

freshly ground black pepper

1½ tablespoons olive oil

1 large egg, separated

pinch sugar

1½ tablespoons vodka

½ cup (125 ml/4 fl oz) cold water

Sift the flour and salt into a large bowl. Make a well in the centre, then individually add oil, egg yolk, sugar, vodka and water, mixing thoroughly after each addition. Stir until smooth, then cover and refrigerate for 2 hours.

Whisk egg white until stiff peaks form, then fold into the batter.

Heat oil in a deep pan until a haze begins to rise. Dip each leaf into the batter and drop into the hot oil. Fry about one minute, turning once. Remove with a slotted spoon, and drain on an oven tray lined with paper towels. Keep hot.

Serve sprinkled with sea salt and accompanied by lime wedges.

BOCCONCINI PRESERVED IN OLIVE OIL

Bocconcini are small balls of mozzarella cheese. There are several ways to serve them: with bruschetta; as part of an antipasta plate; in salads; and sliced with pasta.

500 g (1 lb) bocconcini, drained (see note)

4 sprigs fresh chervil, rinsed and dried

4 sprigs fresh thyme, rinsed and dried

1 sprig fresh rosemary, rinsed and dried

2 to 3 cups (500 to 750 ml/16 to 24 fl oz) extra-virgin olive oil

Place cheese and herbs in a sterilized clip- or screw-top glass jar. Pour in enough olive oil to cover. Seal.

Refrigerate for at least one week, but the longer the better before using.

Note: Small rounds of goat's cheese, cubes of ricotta da tavola (a firm Italian ricotta), feta, or farmer's cheese can also be preserved in this way, using herbs of your choice.

DEEP-FRIED SAGE LEAVES

BRUSCHETTA WITH GRILLED EGGPLANT AND PRESERVED BOCCONCINI

SERVES 6

This recipe can also be made using fresh bocconcini, goat's cheese, ricotta da tavola or farmer's cheese, and fresh olive oil.

- 1 eggplant (aubergine), about 500 g (1 lb), cut into 12 mm (½ in) slices
- ½ cup (125 ml/4 fl oz) olive oil, or oil from a jar of preserved bocconcini (recipe, page 24)
- 2 to 3 tablespoons chopped chervil
- 6 preserved bocconcini
- 1 bunch rocket (arugula)
- 12 thin slices prosciutto
- 1 red or yellow capsicum (sweet pepper), roasted and peeled, and cut into 6 mm (¼ in) strips (see note, page 21)

BRUSCHETTA

- 1 day-old loaf crusty Italian bread, cut into 12 mm (½ in) slices
- 2 cloves garlic, crushed, and finely chopped
- 1 teaspoon sea salt
- 1 cup (250 ml/8 fl oz) oil from preserved bocconcini (see recipe page 24)

DRESSING

- ½ cup (125 ml/4 fl oz) walnut oil
- 2 tablespoons verjuice (see note), or white wine vinegar
- 1 tablespoon snipped chives
- freshly ground black pepper

Preheat oven to 150°C (300°F).

To make bruschetta, combine garlic, salt and oil, and brush both sides of bread with this. (Use extra plain olive oil to supplement this, if required.)

Place bread on rack over an oven tray and bake for 20 minutes, or until crisp and pale golden.

Remove from oven, cool, and store in an airtight container until required.

Sprinkle eggplant slices with salt, and leave for 30 minutes.

Rinse eggplant with cold water, and pat dry. Brush both sides lightly with olive oil, then grill on a hot grill pan or the barbecue, about 3 to 4 minutes on each side.

Transfer eggplant to a warm dish and sprinkle with chervil. Keep warm.

Place 12 to 18 slices bruschetta on a grill tray, slice half a bocconcini onto each and place under a hot grill for 2 to 3 minutes, until bocconcini melts a little.

Combine dressing ingredients.

To serve, place 2 to 3 slices of bruschetta on each plate and arrange arugula, prosciutto, capsicum and eggplant to one side. Sprinkle with dressing.

Note: Verjuice is unfermented juice of white grapes.

CHERVIL

Chervil is an annual. Its lacy fern-like leaves are a light bright green when young and a soft dark pink colour when mature. The leaves are quite decorative as well as having great culinary value. Chervil can grow 30 to 45 cm (12 to 18 in) or more in height. It is native to Eastern Europe and has now spread throughout the world; it is especially popular in France where it is known as *cerfeuil* and it is one of the *fines herbes* mixtures.

On chervil broth: 'Instead of boiling your Chervil, pound it, and take about a glass of its Juice, mix it with your Broth, whilst it is hot, but not boiling, lest the Juice loses its Taste and Quality. This Broth is very cooling though it does not look pleasing to the Eye, by reason of its Greenness; but it has more Vertue in the Spring, to sweeten and purify the Blood, than in any other Season.'

—*The Receipt Book of Vincent La Chapelle, Chief Cook to the Prince of Orange, 1774*

STUFFED NASTURTIUM LEAVES

SERVES 6 TO 8

24 to 30 nasturtium leaves, well washed

I cup (250 g/8 oz) creamed cottage cheese or farmer's cheese

I clove garlic, crushed with a pinch of salt

freshly ground black pepper

juice ½ lemon

6 tablespoons chopped fresh herbs (e.g. parsley, basil, oregano)

¼ bunch chives, snipped

paprika, to sprinkle

nasturtium flowers, to garnish

Shake the leaves dry.

In a bowl combine cheese, garlic, lemon juice and herbs. Add pepper to taste.

Spread a thick layer of cheese mixture over one half of each leaf. Fold the other half of the leaf over and press lightly to seal. Do not completely close. Lightly sprinkle exposed cheese with paprika. Chill.

Serve garnished with nasturtium flowers.

PARSLEY

Parsley is one of the first herbs to appear in spring and so, for centuries, has been used in the Jewish Passover meal—or seder—to symbolize a new start.

DILL-MARINATED OCEAN TROUT

Use this fish in salads, or with bread and mustard sauce (recipe follows).

3 tablespoons sea salt

3 tablespoons raw sugar

2 tablespoons white peppercorns, crushed

I bunch fresh dill, roughly snipped

finely grated rind of 2 limes

2 ocean trout fillets, skin on

Combine salt, sugar and peppercorns. Spread a large sheet of foil on work surface and sprinkle with one third of the salt mixture, one third of the dill, and one third of the rind.

Lay one fillet, skin side down, on this, then sprinkle similarly, with another third of the salt mixture, dill and rind.

Place remaining fillet on top, and sprinkle with remaining salt mixture, dill and rind.

Wrap fish securely in foil. Place package in a baking tin. Place another, slightly smaller baking tin, or one which fits inside the first, on top. Place weights (cans of food are suitable) in the second tin and refrigerate for two days, turning the foil parcel several times.

Remove fish from foil, and scrape off herbs and seasonings.

Place fillets skin-side down on a board. With a large, smooth-bladed sharp knife, slice into the flesh diagonally across the fillet, starting at the thick end. Slice through until the knife reaches the skin, angle the knife slightly towards the thick end of the fillet, and cut flesh off the skin. Repeat, slicing thinly. Discard skin.

MUSTARD SAUCE

Combine equal quantities of brown sugar and Dijon mustard, to form a thin paste.

DILL

Fresh dill sprigs make an attractive and flavoursome accompaniment to vegetables, meat, cheese, eggs and fish. Dill is a traditional condiment in Scandinavian cuisine, notably with the raw fish dish gravlax, and with dishes featuring sour cream, such as potato salad. Dill leaves are a delicious garnish for mayonnaise and for recipes with a yoghurt or cream-cheese base.

Dill is a lucky plant and, in some European countries, a bride will place a sprig of dill and a pinch of salt in one of her shoes on her wedding day to ensure her marriage is a happy one.

Salads, Side Dishes and Light Meals

Beetroot and Borage Salad

**Chicory Salad with
Summer Savory Dressing**

Potato, Sage and Thyme Frittata

Pan-fried Potato Cake

Smoked Eggplant and Yoghurt Salad

Chicken, Avocado and Pawpaw Salad

Roasted Capsicums and Spanish Onions

Roasted Tomato Relish

Mango Salsa

Seafood Pizza with Pesto

Raita

**Parmesan and Herb Pikelets with
Scrambled Eggs and Prosciutto**

**Dill Crepes with Rollmops
and Red Cabbage**

Harlequin Pizza

Oven-baked Desiree Potatoes

Pork Pies with Savoury Herbed Puff Pastry

Savoury Herbed Puff Pastry

Parsley Honey

Potato and Parmesan Tart

Fresh Herb and Prosciutto Tart

Whiting Fillets in Sage Beer Batter

**Mussels with Creamy Saffron
and Basil Sauce**

Minted Spinach Couscous

WHITING FILLETS IN SAGE BEER BATTER, PAGE 43, WITH ROASTED
TOMATO RELISH, PAGE 35, AND PAN-FRIED POTATO CAKE, PAGE 33
(Le Creuset frying pan from J.D. Milner & Assoc.)

BEETROOT AND BORAGE SALAD

SERVES 6 TO 8

8 medium beetroot

½ cup (125 ml/4 fl oz) verjuice (see note, page 26), honey mead vinegar, or cider vinegar

1 clove garlic, crushed

2 teaspoons honey

1 medium Spanish onion, finely chopped

1 bunch chives, snipped

1 bunch borage (about 10 leaves), sliced

200 ml (6½ fl oz) crème fraîche

1 cup (250 ml/8 fl oz) natural yoghurt

salt and freshly ground black pepper

Boil whole beetroot for about 30 minutes. Meanwhile, combine the verjuice, garlic and honey.

Rinse the beetroot under cold running water and rub off skins.

Cut beetroot into 12 mm (½ in) dice.

While the beetroot is still warm, add to combined verjuice, garlic and honey, and marinate for 30 minutes.

Combine with remaining ingredients, add salt and pepper to taste, mix well, and chill before serving.

BASIL

To preserve basil leaves whole: cover the herbs with oil or vinegar, cap tightly and leave on a sunny windowsill for two weeks, shaking occasionally.

CHICORY SALAD WITH SUMMER SAVORY DRESSING

SERVES 8

The herbs in this salad can be varied to whatever is available. The opal (or purple) basil provides an attractive colour contrast, so use it if possible.

1 tablespoon macadamia or Dijon mustard

1 egg yolk

1 tablespoon Cognac

2 tablespoons verjuice (see note, page 26), or white wine vinegar

1 teaspoon finely chopped summer savory

¼ cup macadamia oil

salt and freshly ground white pepper

young tender leaves from 1 head of chicory, washed, dried and chilled

leaves from 6 sprigs opal basil, torn

leaves from 4 sprigs summer savory

leaves from ½ bunch watercress

½ cup torn lovage leaves

1 bunch chives, chopped into 12 mm (½ in) lengths

Blend the mustard with the egg yolk. Add Cognac, verjuice and summer savory and blend until smooth. Add oil in a slow, steady stream, blending constantly until oil is completely incorporated. Add salt and pepper to taste.

Place salad greens on a serving platter or in a bowl. Chill. Toss with dressing just before serving.

BEETROOT AND BORAGE SALAD

POTATO, SAGE AND THYME FRITTATA

SERVES 6

1 kg (2 lb) Pink Eye or Desiree potatoes, scrubbed and cut into 12 mm (½ in) dice

8 eggs, beaten

2 tablespoons crème fraîche or sour cream

2 tablespoons finely chopped sage

1 tablespoon thyme leaves

salt and freshly crushed green peppercorns

30 g (1 oz) butter

Preheat oven to 180°C (350°F).

Steam potatoes until tender.

Beat eggs and crème fraîche together until light and fluffy. Combine with steamed potatoes, herbs and peppercorns.

Melt butter in a deep, cast-iron frying pan or heavy frying pan with removable or heat-proof handle. Pour in frittata mixture, cook over a medium heat for 5 minutes or until the base is brown.

Transfer pan to oven and cook for 10 minutes, or until centre is just set.

Finish off under the grill, to brown top.

(Alternatively, cook frittata on one side until browned, place a dinner plate over the top and invert frying pan so frittata falls onto plate. Replace pan over heat and slide frittata, cooked side up, back into pan to cook the base.)

Serve hot, cut into wedges.

POTATO, SAGE AND THYME FRITTATA
(Le Creuset frying pan from J.D. Milner & Assoc.)

PAN-FRIED POTATO CAKE

SERVES 6

450 g (1 lb) old potatoes

1 clove garlic, crushed

1 onion, grated

1 tablespoon finely chopped parsley

1 tablespoon finely chopped chervil

salt

oil for shallow frying (see note)

Peel and grate potatoes and place in a colander to drain.

Squeeze out as much liquid as possible from the potatoes, then combine with remaining ingredients, except oil.

Pour oil into a heavy based frying pan to a depth of about 6 mm (¼ in). Heat until a haze is just beginning to become visible, then add the potato mixture. Quickly spread out the mixture to coat the pan, and cook over a moderately hot heat until browned underneath.

Invert potato cake onto a dinner plate and slide back into the pan to cook the top.

Serve immediately, cut into wedges.

Note: A good oil for this recipe is walnut or macadamia oil.

PARSLEY

For a pleasant and unusual vegetable side dish, bake the roots of parsley and serve with butter and lemon juice—they taste rather like carrots.

SMOKED EGGPLANT AND YOGHURT SALAD

SERVES 6

Serve with Roti (recipe, page 80) or flat breads, or to accompany a spicy meal.

- **1 large eggplant (aubergine)**
- **1 large tomato, peeled, seeded and chopped**
- **½ cup finely chopped spring onions**
- **300 ml (10 fl oz) plain yoghurt**
- **⅓ cup (80 ml/2½ fl oz) sour cream**
- **sea salt**
- **3 tablespoons vegetable oil**
- **1 tablespoon shredded fresh ginger root**
- **½ teaspoon cayenne**
- **½ cup finely chopped coriander**
- **1½ teaspoons cumin seeds, roasted (see note), and crushed**
- **paprika or cayenne for garnish**

Preheat oven to 225°C (440°F).

Make a small X cut in base of eggplant and place it on a rack in a baking tray. Roast for 50 to 60 minutes. Remove from oven, and leave to cool until easy to handle.

Carefully peel the skin off the eggplant. Chop flesh.

Combine eggplant with tomato, spring onion, yoghurt, sour cream and salt to taste.

Combine the remaining ingredients and stir into eggplant mixture. Spoon into a shallow dish and sprinkle with paprika or cayenne.

Note: To roast cumin seeds, place on a shallow dish and microwave on high for 3 minutes, or bake in a hot oven (200°C/400°F) for 5 minutes, stirring once.

Hint: A delicious smoky flavour is obtained if the eggplant is roasted in a covered barbecue or over a wood fire.

CHICKEN, AVOCADO, AND PAWPAW SALAD

SERVES 6

- **4 chicken fillets, skin removed**
- **1 stalk lemon grass, crushed**
- **3 kaffir lime leaves (fresh or dried)**
- **500 g (1 lb) smoked chicken meat**
- **1 pawpaw (papaya), peeled, seeded, and cut into 12 mm (½ in) dice**
- **2 avocados, peeled, pitted, and cut into 12 mm (½ in) dice**
- **½ cup coarsely chopped roasted walnuts (see note)**
- **1 cup watercress leaves**
- **½ cup torn sorrel leaves**
- **12 perilla leaves**

WALNUT AND LIME DRESSING

- **⅓ cup (80 ml/2½ fl oz) fresh lime juice**
- **¾ cup (190 ml/6 fl oz) walnut oil**
- **finely grated rind of 1 lime**
- **¼ teaspoon salt**
- **¼ teaspoon freshly ground black pepper**

Place chicken fillets, lemon grass and kaffir lime leaves in a deep frying pan and add enough cold water to just cover. Bring to a simmer over a moderate heat and poach gently for five minutes.

Remove the chicken fillets from the poaching liquid and drain. (Strain and reserve the poaching liquid for use as chicken stock, especially where Asian flavours are required.)

Cut poached and smoked chicken meat into thin slices.

Combine chicken with pawpaw, avocado, walnuts and herbs. Arrange on individual plates.

Combine dressing ingredients and pour over salad.

Serve immediately.

Note: To roast walnuts, spread nuts on a shallow dish and microwave on high for 3 to 5 minutes, or bake in a hot oven (200°C/400°F) for 5 to 8 minutes, stirring once.

SORREL

The Romans were thought to be the first to cultivate sorrel for culinary use. They used it as a condiment for meat, the sharp somewhat citrusy flavour probably helping to digest rich meats and game. Roman soldiers on guard duty chewed sorrel leaves to stave off thirst, a tip still mentioned in almanacs and books on natural remedies.

The use of sorrel reached its peak during Tudor times, when it was widely used as a pot herb, as a 'salading', as a filling for tarts, and also as an ingredient in all manner of vegetable dishes or 'pottages'. The leaves were also used as a cooling, protective herb for cheeses and butters.

ROASTED CAPSICUMS AND SPANISH ONIONS

SERVES 6

2 large Spanish onions, peeled and cut into eighths

1 large red and 2 large yellow capsicums (sweet peppers), seeded and cut into 2.5 cm (1 in) strips

1 tablespoon olive oil

3 sprigs fresh rosemary

3 tablespoons freshly chopped Italian parsley

Preheat oven to 200°C (400°F).

Place onion and capsicum into a roasting pan. Rub with olive oil and bake for 20 minutes, stirring occasionally.

Stir in rosemary and parsley and bake for a further 15 minutes.

Serve hot or at room temperature.

ROASTED TOMATO RELISH

MAKES ABOUT 2 CUPS (500 ML/16 FL OZ)

1 kg (2 lb) egg tomatoes

1 medium Spanish onion, finely chopped

2 tablespoons chopped chervil

2 tablespoons chopped Italian parsley

1 tablespoon thyme leaves

½ cup (125 ml/4 fl oz) walnut oil

¼ cup (60 ml/2 fl oz) balsamic vinegar

salt and freshly ground black pepper

Preheat oven to 160°C (325°F).

Slice tomatoes in half lengthways and place in one layer, cut-side up, in a shallow roasting dish. Roast for 45 to 60 minutes.

Chop tomatoes roughly and combine with remaining ingredients.

MANGO SALSA

MAKES ABOUT 2 CUPS (500 ML/16 FL OZ)

½ cup (125 ml/4 fl oz) verjuice (see note, page 26) or white wine vinegar

2 tablespoons raw sugar

2 cloves garlic, bruised

5 cm (2 in) piece fresh ginger root, peeled and quartered

2 teaspoons coriander seeds

2 teaspoons black peppercorns

2 semi-ripe mangoes, peeled, flesh cut away from stones and diced

1 small red banana chilli (chili pepper), finely diced

½ small Spanish onion, finely diced

1 small fresh red chilli (chili pepper), finely sliced (to give about 1 tablespoon)

½ teaspoon ground cumin

¼ cup freshly chopped coriander

8 mint leaves, torn

Combine verjuice with sugar, garlic, ginger, coriander seeds and peppercorns in a small non-corrosive saucepan and stir over a medium heat until the sugar dissolves. Simmer 5 minutes.

Turn off heat. Remove 1 clove of the garlic and 1 piece of the ginger and chop finely.

Combine mango in a bowl with finely chopped reserved garlic and ginger. Add remaining ingredients to the mango mixture.

Heat verjuice mixture in saucepan until boiling, then strain over the mango mixture. Transfer to a glass container, seal, and stand in a cool place until required.

SEAFOOD PIZZA WITH PESTO

SERVES 6 TO 8

DOUGH

1 sachet (7 g/¼ oz) dry yeast

350 ml (12 oz) warm water

300 g (10 oz) unbleached bread flour, and extra for flouring the work surface

60 g (2 oz) finely ground cornmeal

salt and freshly ground black pepper

FILLING

½ cup pesto (recipe, page 77)

450 g (15 oz) blue-eye cod fillet, cut into 2 cm (¾ in) dice

8 scallops

500 g (1 lb) medium green prawns (shrimps), shelled and deveined

8 sundried tomatoes, roughly chopped

200 g (6½ oz) grated mozzarella cheese

basil, for garnish

TO MAKE THE DOUGH

Line a 25 cm (10 in) pizza tin with baking paper (so pizza will be easy to slide off onto serving platter).

Dissolve yeast in the warm water. Combine remaining ingredients in a separate large bowl and stir in yeast mixture. Mix well to form a dough.

Turn out the dough onto a floured work surface and knead for 5 minutes. Roll out dough to line the pizza tin.

TO MAKE THE FILLING

Spread pesto over the pizza base. Arrange fish, scallops, prawns, and tomatoes on top, then cover with cheese.

Preheat oven to 200°C (400°F). While the oven is heating, cover the pizza and stand it in a warm, draught-free position for 30 minutes.

Cook pizza for 20 to 25 minutes, or until base is just golden.

Serve immediately, garnished with basil.

RAITA

MAKES ABOUT 2 CUPS (500 ML/16 FL OZ)

Serve as an accompaniment to curries, with fried food, as a dip for vegetables, or with bread.

300 ml (10 fl oz) plain yoghurt

150 ml (5 fl oz) sour cream

2 teaspoons finely chopped mint leaves

1 tablespoon finely chopped coriander leaves

1 teaspoon cumin seeds, roasted (see note, page 34), and ground

¼ teaspoon cayenne (optional)

2 teaspoons sugar

salt and freshly ground black pepper

½ cup finely diced cucumber or tomato flesh

paprika, for garnish

Combine all ingredients (except paprika), and cover. Chill thoroughly.

Raita will keep, refrigerated, for up to 2 days.

SEAFOOD PIZZA WITH PESTO
(Glasses, board, cutlery and jugs from The Bay Tree)

PARMESAN AND HERB PIKELETS WITH SCRAMBLED EGGS AND PROSCIUTTO

SERVES 6

PIKELETS

1 cup (140 g/5 oz) self-raising flour

pinch of salt

2 eggs, lightly beaten

¾ cup (180 ml/6 fl oz) milk

3 tablespoons sour cream

30 g (1 oz) butter, melted, and extra for greasing pan

⅓ cup grated Parmesan cheese

2 teaspoons rosemary leaves

2 tablespoons snipped chives

2 tablespoons chopped parsley

SCRAMBLED EGGS

125 g butter

10 eggs

½ cup (125 ml/4 fl oz) cream

2 tablespoons sour cream

1 tablespoon lemon thyme leaves

salt and freshly ground black pepper

18 very thin slices prosciutto

TO MAKE THE PIKELETS

Sift flour with a pinch of salt into a large bowl. Make a well in centre and add combined egg, milk, sour cream, and melted butter. Mix to a smooth batter, stir in cheese and herbs.

Heat a heavy frying pan or cast-iron griddle and grease lightly. Pour quarter-cup quantities of the mixture into pan and cook over a moderate heat until surface begins to bubble. Turn just before bubbles burst and cook other side until golden.

Remove from pan and stack on a clean tea-towel (dish cloth) on a wire rack.

Repeat with remaining mixture. (There should be sufficient mixture to make 12 pikelets.)

TO MAKE THE SCRAMBLED EGGS

Melt butter in a heavy based pan over a low heat.

Whisk eggs, cream and sour cream until fluffy.

Mix in lemon thyme, and salt and freshly ground black pepper to taste.

Pour mixture into pan and cook over a low heat until beginning to set at sides. Stir gently with a fork, pushing from the outside into centre, until eggs are just set. Remove from heat.

FOR PROSCIUTTO

Dry-fry the prosciutto in a heavy based frying pan, or grill, or bake in a hot oven until crisp.

To serve, place two pikelets on warmed plates with scrambled eggs and three slices of prosciutto each. Serve hot.

DILL CREPES WITH ROLLMOPS AND RED CABBAGE

SERVES 4

1 cup (125 g/4 oz) plain flour

pinch of salt

1 egg plus 1 egg yolk

1 cup (250 ml/8 fl oz) milk

1 tablespoon melted butter, and extra for greasing the pan

½ cup snipped dill, and extra sprigs for garnish

1 can (425 g/14 oz) red cabbage

250 g (8 oz) rollmops, drained and chopped

4 pickled onions, sliced

300 ml (10 fl oz) sour cream

Sieve flour and salt into a bowl. Add egg, yolk and half the milk. Beat thoroughly until smooth, then mix in remaining milk and the butter. Beat until bubbly, then stir in the dill. Pour into a jug, and cover. Refrigerate for 30 minutes.

Cook crepes in a heated, lightly greased pancake pan. (There should be sufficient mixture for 8 crepes.) Stack crepes as you cook them, separating each with plastic wrap or baking paper.

Preheat oven to 180°C (350°F).

Spread about 3 tablespoons red cabbage in centre of each crepe, top with some chopped rollmop, pickled onion and 1 tablespoon sour cream. Roll crepes to form neat parcels.

Place crepes onto an oven tray and reheat for a few minutes, to warm through.

Allow two crepes for each person. Before serving, top with sour cream and garnish with dill sprigs. Serve immediately.

> ### CHIVES
> Pickle tiny chive bulbs as a gourmet treat for anyone who enjoys savoury foods.

HARLEQUIN PIZZA

SERVES 4 TO 6

DOUGH

20 g (⅔ oz) compressed yeast

pinch of salt

½ teaspoon sugar

150 ml (5 fl oz) warm water

1 tablespoon olive oil, plus extra

300 g (10 oz) plain (all purpose) white flour

FILLING

8 egg tomatoes

2 large red capsicums (sweet peppers)

2 large yellow capsicums (sweet peppers)

4 rounds marinated feta (about 250 g/8 oz)

1 cup pesto (recipe, page 77)

8 thin slices proscuitto, halved horizontally

4 sprigs fresh thyme

4 sprigs fresh rosemary

4 sprigs fresh marjoram

4 sprigs fresh oregano

freshly ground black pepper

TO MAKE THE DOUGH

Preheat oven to 150°C (300°F).

Dissolve yeast, salt and sugar in the warm water. Stir in the tablespoon of olive oil.

Mound flour onto a work surface and make a well in the centre. Add yeast mixture drop by drop into the centre, mixing in flour with your fingertips until all moisture is absorbed. Knead dough until smooth and of 'earlobe' texture.

Form into a ball and place in a large, lightly oiled bowl. Turn dough to coat with oil, cover bowl with a clean tea towel and leave in a warm (not less than 20°C/68°F), draught-free position until almost tripled in bulk, about 1 hour.

While the dough is rising, prepare the filling.

TO MAKE THE FILLING

Halve tomatoes lengthwise and place on a lightly oiled oven tray. Bake at 150°C (300°F) for 1 hour, or until juices are beginning to dry.

While the tomatoes are cooking, halve and seed capsicums. Rub skins lightly with olive oil and place on a shallow oven tray. Bake in hotter part of the oven, with the tomatoes, until skins of the capsicums are blackened and blistered. Remove from oven and transer to a bowl. Cover, and stand for 15 minutes.

Peel skins from the capsicums. Keeping red and yellow capsicums separate, slice flesh into 6 mm (¼ in) strips. Return strips to oven tray and cooking juices. Stand at room temperature until required.

TO COMPLETE

Increase oven temperature to 230°C (450°F).

Roll dough into a ball and place on a lightly oiled pizza tray. Ease dough to edge of tray by pressing gently with your fingertips and the heel of your hand. Make the edges of the pizza base slightly thicker than the centre, to retain filling.

Cut feta rounds in half to form crescents, then cut each crescent horizontally into 3 or 4 slices.

Spread three-quarters of the pesto over the pizza base, to within 2.5 cm (1 in) of the edge.

Arrange tomato on one quarter of the base, and sprinkle with thyme.

Arrange red capsicum slices on the opposite quarter, and sprinkle with rosemary.

Combine yellow capsicum with the prosciutto, and arrange in one quarter. Sprinkle with marjoram and oregano.

In remaining quarter, arrange feta slices, and drizzle with remaining pesto.

Drizzle capsicum cooking juices and grind black pepper over the entire surface.

Bake for 15 to 20 minutes, or until base has risen and is crisp.

Serve hot or at room temperature.

OVEN-BAKED DESIREE POTATOES

SERVES 6

6 Desiree potatoes, washed (see note)

1 tablespoon olive oil

1 tablespoon sea salt

6 cloves garlic, peeled

4 sprigs fresh rosemary

Preheat oven to 200°C (400°F).

Cut unpeeled potatoes into 12 mm (½ in) slices. Place in one layer in a roasting pan and rub with oil. Sprinkle with sea salt. Add garlic and rosemary and bake for 20 to 30 minutes, until golden. Turn occasionally and shake pan to prevent sticking.

Note: Pontiac potatoes are also suitable.

PORK PIES WITH SAVOURY HERBED PUFF PASTRY

SERVES 6

- **1 portion (500 g/1 lb) savoury herbed puff pastry (recipe follows)**
- **butter or oil for greasing pie tins**
- **500 g (1 lb) minced lean pork**
- **2 teaspoons ground cumin**
- **1 tablespoon fresh thyme leaves**
- **3 cloves garlic, crushed**
- **1 teaspoon salt**
- **1 teaspoon freshly ground white pepper**
- **1 egg yolk**

Place a large baking slide in oven and heat oven to 190°C (375°F). Grease six pie tins (10 cm/4 in).

Roll half the pastry out onto a lightly floured surface, to a thickness of 3 mm (⅛ in), and line the pie tins.

Prick bases of the pie shells with a fork. Press the pastry scraps together. Chill the pie shells and scraps while preparing filling.

Combine remaining ingredients, except egg yolk. Spoon the mixture into the pie shells.

Roll out remaining pastry and scraps, and cut circles slightly larger than the pie tins. Brush edges with cold water and place pastry rounds on top of pies, pressing edges gently to seal.

Whisk egg yolk with a pinch of salt and brush tops of pies, taking care

PORK PIES WITH SAVOURY HERBED PUFF PASTRY
(Napkin from Les Olivades. Armetale Wilton kettle from The Bay Tree)

not to let any of the egg drip on to the cut edges of the pastry.

Place tins on the hot baking slide and bake for 25 to 30 minutes, or until pastry is puffed and golden.

Serve hot.

SAVOURY HERBED PUFF PASTRY

MAKES 1 KG (2 LBS)

- **500 g (1 lb) unsalted butter**
- **500 g (1 lb) plain flour**
- **1¼ cups (310 ml/10 fl oz) cream**
- **1 teaspoon salt**
- **1 cup leaves of fresh herbs (see note)**

Beat the butter with an electric mixer until smooth. Add ½ cup (60 g/2 oz) of the flour, mix until smooth. Scrape this mixture onto a large piece of baking paper and shape into a square 12.5 cm x 12.5cm (5 in x 5 in). Wrap and chill.

Combine remaining flour, cream and salt. Mix to a smooth dough, but don't overmix. Shape into a ball, wrap, and chill for 15 minutes.

Roll dough ball into a rectangle 30 cm x 15 cm (12 in x 6 in). Place the butter square in the centre of the rectangle and fold dough over to completely encase it. Press edges together, sealing as well as possible. Wrap and chill to bring both dough and butter to same temperature.

Roll pastry on a lightly floured surface, into a long rectangle, about 1 cm (⅜ in) thick. Sprinkle herbs over the dough then fold dough in three. Turn dough 90 degrees, roll again into a long rectangle, 1 cm

(⅜ in) thick. Scatter more herbs over surface, and fold again, neatly to keep edges in line and butter evenly distributed between layers. Wrap, and chill for 1 hour.

Repeat the rolling, sprinkling of herbs, folding and chilling process two more times (to give a total of six rollings).

After the sixth rolling, cut the pastry into two equal portions. Wrap separately, and chill until required.

Note: Your choice of herbs (for example, chervil, sage, dill, summer savory, tarragon, snipped chives) will depend on the intended final use of the pastry.

PARSLEY HONEY

MAKES 3 X 450 G (1 LB) JARS

Use as an accompaniment to cold meats, or as a drink base (mix with hot water).

- **125 g (4 oz) fresh parsley, chopped**
- **900 g (1 lb 14 oz) raw sugar**
- **3½ cups (875 ml/28 fl oz) hot water**

Combine parsley with the hot water, cover, and leave to infuse for 20 minutes.

Bring parsley infusion to the boil. (The colour should drain from the parsley into the water.)

Strain off liquid to a clean pan and add sugar. Heat to dissolve the sugar, stirring constantly, then boil until mixture begins to thicken.

Remove from heat and pour into warm, dry, sterilized glass jars. Seal.

POTATO AND PARMESAN TART

SERVES 6 TO 8

- **125 g (4 oz) butter, and extra for greasing the tart pan**
- **1 onion, sliced very thinly**
- **3 cloves garlic, chopped**
- **10 potatoes, peeled and sliced very thinly**
- **½ cup chopped herbs (chervil, parsley, chives, dill)**
- **1 tablespoon freshly ground pink peppercorns**
- **200 g (7 oz) freshly grated Parmesan cheese**

Preheat oven to 190°C (375°F). Grease a 23 cm (9 in) springform tin.

Melt butter in a deep frying pan. Add onion and garlic and cook over a moderate heat until soft. Add potatoes and turn gently to coat with butter. Remove from heat.

Layer potatoes, herbs, peppercorns and Parmesan into the greased springform tin. Finish with herbs and Parmesan.

Bake for 40 minutes, or until the potatoes are tender and the tart is golden. Remove from oven and stand 10 minutes.

Remove from tin and cut into wedges. Serve.

Note: Serve as an accompaniment to barbecues or with cold meats and pickled onions.

FRESH HERB AND PROSCIUTTO TART

SERVES 6

PASTRY

- **150 g (5 oz) unbleached flour**
- **90 g (3 oz) butter**
- **1 egg yolk**
- **1 tablespoon lemon juice**

FILLING

- **4 eggs**
- **150 ml (5 fl oz) cream**
- **250 g (8 oz) farmer's cheese, crumbled (see note, page 22)**
- **60 g (2 oz) mixed fresh herbs of your choice (e.g. parsley, chives, chervil, sorrel, oregano), finely chopped**
- **salt and freshly ground black pepper**
- **6 thin slices prosciutto**

TO MAKE THE THE PASTRY

Sift flour with a pinch of salt into a large bowl. Rub in butter until mixture resembles fine breadcrumbs, then stir in combined yolk and lemon juice. Add a little chilled water if mixture is too dry. Form into a disc, wrap and refrigerate for 30 minutes.

Preheat oven to 200°C (400°F).

Roll dough to line a buttered 23 cm (9 in) tart tin.

Refrigerate the pastry case for 15 minutes, then prick base lightly. Line with baking paper or foil and fill with baking weights, dried beans or rice. Bake blind for 10 to 15 minutes. Remove weights and baking paper, return to oven until pastry is set but not coloured, about 5 minutes.

PARSLEY

Parsley has been widely grown and used for thousands of years, as a garnish and flavouring and as a medicinal tonic herb. It was probably indigenous to the Mediterranean region and taken abroad by the Romans. It is now naturalized throughout the world, especially in maritime areas and limestone or rocky locations.

CHIVES

Chives go well with fish and chicken and, along with chervil, tarragon and parsley, they make up the traditional French fines herbes mixture. They are said to stimulate the appetite and to make barbecued meats easier to digest, by 'cutting through' the fat of lamb or beef.

Remove from oven and reduce temperature to 190°C (375°F).

TO MAKE THE FILLING

Beat eggs and cream. Stir in crumbled cheese and herbs then season to taste.

Pour filling into pastry case. Arrange prosciutto slices on top.

Return to oven for 35 to 40 minutes, until the filling is set and the prosciutto is crisp.

Serve warm or at room temperature.

WHITING FILLETS IN SAGE BEER BATTER

SERVES 6 TO 8

Serve with Roasted Tomato Relish (recipe, page 35) or Mango Salsa (recipe, page 35) or fresh lemon and lime wedges.

- **2 cups (250 g/8 oz) self-raising flour**
- **1 teaspoon salt**
- **1½ cups (375 ml/12 fl oz) beer**
- **6 sage leaves, finely chopped**
- **500 g (1 lb) whiting fillets**
- **oil, for deep-frying**

Whisk flour, salt and beer until smooth. Stir in sage.

Heat oil in a deep pot until it reaches 185°C (365°F). Dip whiting fillets in batter, and drop small batches into hot oil. Cook each batch until golden, about 4 minutes. Remove with a slotted spoon, and drain on absorbent paper. Keep warm.

Between cooking each batch, scoop stray bits of batter from the oil and discard.

Serve warm.

MUSSELS WITH CREAMY SAFFRON AND BASIL SAUCE

SERVES 4

- **1.5 kg (3 lb) New Zealand greenlip mussels in the shell, cleaned**
- **3 cups (750 ml/25 fl oz) dry white wine**
- **¼ teaspoon saffron threads**

- **2 tablespoons olive oil**
- **4 golden shallots (French shallots or eschalots), finely chopped**
- **2 cloves garlic, crushed**
- **2 medium zucchini (courgettes), cut into batons 5 cm (2 in) long**
- **4 tomatoes, peeled, seeded, and diced**
- **1 tablespoon tomato paste**
- **60 g (2 oz) butter, cut into small dice**
- **¼ cup (60 ml/2 fl oz) cream**
- **2 tablespoons chopped fresh basil, and 4 sprigs extra for garnish**
- **1 tablespoon snipped chives**
- **salt and pepper**

Place mussels in a large saucepan with wine. Cover, bring to boil, reduce heat and simmer until mussels open, about 5 minutes.

Remove mussels from pan and strain the cooking liquid into a bowl. Reserve.

Remove mussels from shells.

Heat oil in a large frying pan, add shallots and garlic and cook, stirring, over a moderate heat for 5 minutes, or until soft.

Add zucchini and tomato, 2 cups of the reserved stock and the tomato paste. Simmer 5 minutes.

Whisk in butter, piece by piece, then stir in cream and herbs. Add mussels, season with salt and pepper and heat 2 minutes.

Serve immediately, garnished with basil sprigs.

MINTED SPINACH COUSCOUS

SERVES 4

An accompaniment to meat dishes.

- **1 cup (170 g/6 oz) instant couscous**
- **½ teaspoon salt**
- **¾ cup (180 ml/6 fl oz) boiling water**
- **6 sundried tomatoes, chopped**
- **2 tablespoons oil from sundried tomatoes**
- **30 g (1 oz) butter**
- **1 packet (250 g/8 oz) frozen chopped spinach, thawed, and drained**
- **1 tablespoon chopped mint**

Combine couscous and salt in a bowl. Pour water over and stand 5 minutes.

Heat oil and butter in a frying pan. Add couscous and stir over a medium heat for 3 minutes.

Add tomatoes and spinach and cook a further 3 minutes.

Stir in mint and serve hot.

SAGE

Sage is a very ancient herb, having been held in repute as a culinary and medicinal plant since Classical times. Sage grew wild in southern Europe during Roman times and as the soldiers moved into France, Germany and Britain, they took sage with them.

Vegetarian Meals

Herbed Mushroom and Ricotta Loaf

Pissaladière

Herbed Corn Spoonbread

Okra Casserole

Tofu with Snake Beans and Chilli

Herb Pasta with Fennel Cream Sauce

Baked Herb Ricotta

Sesame Cheese Pie

Risotto with Herbs

Cauliflower in Yoghurt

Herbed Saffron Cannelloni with
Ricotta and Sorrel

Wild Mushroom Tart

Gnocchi with Spinach Sauce

Chitchkee

Spinach and Potato Curry

Cabbage and Carrot Bhujia

Herb Butters

HERBED MUSHROOM AND RICOTTA LOAF, PAGE 46, AND BAKED HERB
RICOTTA, PAGE 52

(Board and Primo square platter from The Bay Tree. Pillivuyt plates from Hale
Imports)

HERBED MUSHROOM AND RICOTTA LOAF

MAKES ONE LOAF

Serve with salad or Roasted Tomato Relish (recipe, page 35).

- 1 Italian bread ring
- ½ cup (125 ml/4 fl oz) olive oil
- 500 g (1 lb) ricotta
- 3 eggs
- 500 g (1 lb) field mushrooms, chopped
- 2 teaspoons tinned green peppercorns, drained
- 2 tablespoons capers, drained
- 1 clove garlic, crushed
- 1 cup combined chopped herbs (marjoram, oregano, parsley, chervil, chives, thyme)
- salt and freshly ground black pepper

Preheat oven to 180°C (350°F).

Slice top crust off bread and scoop out soft centre, to form a shell. Brush shell with oil. (You could make breadcrumbs from the left-over centre and freeze for another use.)

Beat ricotta with eggs. Fold in mushrooms, peppercorns, capers, garlic, herbs, and salt and pepper to taste.

Spoon the mixture into the shell. Replace the top crust, brush with oil, and wrap loaf in foil. Bake for 30 minutes.

Remove foil, return loaf to oven, and bake until crisp.

Remove loaf from oven, cool to room temperature, and cut into thick slices with a sharp knife.

PISSALADIERE

SERVES 6

A traditional French savoury tart, often made without capsicum.

FILLING

- 8 medium **Spanish** onions, thinly sliced
- 1 tablespoon olive oil, and 2 tablespoons extra, to serve
- 10 anchovy fillets, roughly chopped
- 1 red and 1 yellow capsicum (sweet pepper), roasted, and cut into strips 12 mm (½ in) wide (see note, page 21)
- 2 teaspoons chopped fresh marjoram
- freshly ground black pepper
- 26 herb-marinated kalamata olives
- 1 clove garlic, crushed

DOUGH

- 7 g (¼ oz) sachet dry yeast
- 300 g (10 oz) unbleached bread flour, and extra for flouring work surface
- 60 g (3 oz) finely ground cornmeal
- salt and freshly ground black pepper

TO MAKE THE FILLING

Cook onion in oil in a covered, heavy based pan over a low heat, for about 30 minutes, or until juices begin to caramelize. Stir occasionally. Remove from heat and stir in anchovies. Cool.

TO MAKE THE DOUGH

Dissolve yeast in 350 ml (11 fl oz) warm water.

In a separate large bowl combine flour, cornmeal, salt and pepper, then stir in yeast mixture. Mix well to form a dough, then turn onto a lightly floured work surface and knead for 5 minutes. Roll out dough

LEMON GRASS

Lemon grass forms large, dense clumps of pale green, aromatic foliage. It has been cultivated in its native India and southeast Asia since very early times. According to legend, as Alexander the Great rode his elephant along the Egyptian border, he was intoxicated by the aroma given off when the grass was crushed by the elephant's thundering feet.

to line a 25 cm (10 in) tart tin.

Spoon onion mixture into tart, cover with a clean tea towel, and stand in a warm, draught-free position for 30 to 40 minutes until the dough has risen. While the dough is rising, preheat oven to 200°C (400°F), and combine garlic with the remaining olive oil and set aside.

Once the dough has risen, arrange capsicum strips over the onion mixture to form a lattice pattern. Place an olive in centre of each square formed.

Bake tart for 20 minutes, or until crust is cooked and golden on edges.

Strain the olive oil to remove the garlic.

While the pissaladière is still warm, cut into slices and drizzle with the strained oil.

HERBED CORN SPOONBREAD

SERVES 6

Serve with Roasted Tomato Relish (recipe, page 35).

- **2½ cups (600 ml/20 fl oz) milk**
- **30 g (1 oz) plus 45 g (1½ oz) butter, and extra for greasing the dish**
- **kernels from 3 ears corn**
- **1 small onion, finely chopped**
- **¼ cup chopped fresh herbs (lemon thyme, dill, chervil)**
- **½ teaspoon salt**
- **1¼ cups (210 g/7 oz) cornmeal**
- **1½ cups (185 g/6 oz) grated cheddar**
- **6 large eggs, at room temperature, separated**
- **2 tablespoons snipped chives**

Heat milk until almost boiling, then cover and set aside until required.

Melt 30 g (1 oz) of the butter in a large saucepan. Add corn and onion, and cook over a medium heat until onion is soft.

Add herbs, salt, and cornmeal, and stir over medium heat for 5 minutes more.

Slowly add hot milk, stirring constantly. Stir in cheese and egg yolks. Cool mixture to room temperature.

Preheat the oven to 220°C (425°F). Grease a 23 cm (9 in) soufflé dish with a little butter, and set aside.

Beat egg whites to firm peaks. Fold into corn mixture and then transfer to the soufflé dish.

Place in the preheated oven, reduce temperature to 190°C (375°F) and bake for 35 to 40 minutes, until puffed and firm.

Dot with the remaining 45 g (1½ oz) butter and sprinkle with chives. Serve immediately.

CHIVES

Chive flowers are edible as well as decorative. In early summer, the round flower heads burst forth in a riot of colour, from purple through to pink, depending on the variety and the soil conditions.

OKRA CASSEROLE

SERVES 6

- **1 eggplant, sliced**
- **2 carrots, peeled and sliced**
- **2 potatoes, peeled and sliced**
- **2 onions, peeled and sliced**
- **¼ cup (60 ml/2 fl oz) olive oil**
- **4 zucchini, sliced**
- **4 tomatoes, sliced**
- **2 cups okra (fresh or tinned), topped and tailed**
- **¼ cup (10 g/⅓ oz) chopped parsley**
- **2 teaspoons oregano**
- **salt and freshly ground black pepper**
- **¼ teaspoon nutmeg**

Sprinkle eggplant with salt. Leave to stand for 30 minutes. Meanwhile, preheat the oven to 190°C (375°F).

Rinse the eggplant, then pat dry.

DILL

To make dill and cauliflower pickle: 'Boil the Colly-flowers till they fall in Pieces; then with some of the Stalk and worst of the Flower, boil it in a part of Liquor till pretty strong. Then being taken off, strain it; and when settled, clean it from the Bottom. Then with Dill, gross pepper, a pretty quantity of Salt, when cold add as much vinegar as will make it sharp, and pour all upon the Colly-flower.'

—John Evelyn, *Acetaria*, 1699

Place carrots and potatoes in boiling water. Simmer for 5 minutes. Drain, and rinse under cold water.

Heat oil, then fry onions until soft. Remove onion, then fry eggplant until golden.

In a deep casserole layer all the vegetables, sprinkling each layer with a little parsley, oregano, salt, pepper and nutmeg.

Cover casserole and bake for one hour, or until tender.

TOFU WITH SNAKE BEANS AND CHILLI

SERVES 4

1 green chilli (chili pepper), chopped

3 tablespoons brown rice vinegar

½ cup (125 ml/4 fl oz) light soy sauce

½ cup (125 ml/4 fl oz) oyster sauce

¼ cup (60 ml/2 fl oz) peanut oil

1 packet (300 g/10 oz) hard tofu, cut into 2 cm (¾ in) cubes

½ cup sesame seeds

2 cloves garlic, crushed

6 spring onions, sliced

1 bunch snake beans, or green beans, cut into 7.5 cm (3 in) lengths

½ cup coriander, chopped

1 stalk lemon grass, lower stem only, stripped and finely chopped

1 bunch baby green bok choy, roughly chopped

Combine the chilli, vinegar, soy sauce and oyster sauce, and set aside.

Heat oil in a wok and add tofu, sesame seeds and garlic. Stir-fry over a high heat until tofu is golden.

Add spring onion, beans, coriander, lemon grass and bok choy. Toss over high heat for 3 to 4 minutes.

Add the chilli mixture, tossing until vegetables are coated and cooked.

TOFU WITH SNAKE BEANS AND CHILLI
(La Luna table and chair from Potter Williams, Pyrmont. Napkin from The Bay Tree)

HERB PASTA WITH FENNEL CREAM SAUCE

SERVES 6

HERB PASTA

4 cups (500 g/16 oz) unbleached bread flour

3 to 4 eggs

½ cup fennel leaves (no hard stalks)

walnut oil

½ cup coarsely chopped roasted walnuts (see note, page 34)

FENNEL CREAM SAUCE

2 medium bulbs fennel, washed

2 onions, peeled and coarsely chopped

2 cloves garlic, peeled and crushed

1½ cups (375 ml/12 fl oz) dry white wine

1 cup (250 ml/8 fl oz) water

3 egg yolks

¾ cup (180 ml/6 fl oz) cream

salt and freshly ground pepper

TO MAKE THE PASTA

Make a mound of the flour on work surface and make a well in the centre. Break three of the eggs into the well. Using the tip of a long metal spatula, break up the eggs, and mix a little flour into them. Then, using the long edge of the spatula, bring the flour from the outer edge of the pile into the well, mixing as you go. Continue until all the flour is dampened.

If mixture seems very dry, break the remaining egg into it.

Knead lightly to form a ball. Roll in pasta machine, or with a long rolling-pin, until the thickness of lasagne (about 2 mm/¹⁄₁₂ in).

Cut pasta into two equal sized pieces. Scatter ¼ cup of the fennel leaves evenly over one piece. Place remaining piece of pasta on top, pressing gently together. Roll again 2 to 3 times, or until the pieces are blended.

Cut into fettucine (or into other shapes for other recipes).

TO MAKE THE SAUCE

Coarsely chop one fennel bulb and thickly slice the other.

Place chopped fennel in saucepan with onion and garlic. Add wine and water, and bring to a boil over a medium heat. Reduce heat, and simmer until fennel and onion are soft. Remove from heat and cool.

Strain, reserving both the fennel mixture and the liquid.

Boil liquid until reduced by one third. Remove from heat and stir in combined egg yolks and cream. Add salt and pepper to taste. Stir over a moderate heat for 5 minutes.

Add reserved vegetables.

TO COMPLETE

Drop pasta and remaining sliced fennel into a large pot of boiling water, to which a few drops of walnut oil have been added. Cook for 4 minutes.

Drain, and sprinkle with roasted walnuts and remaining ¼ cup of fennel leaves. Serve immediately.

HERB PASTA WITH FENNEL CREAM SAUCE

BAKED HERB RICOTTA

SERVES 6 TO 8

To accompany crusty bread or bruschetta. Serve with a crisp green salad or with roasted capsicum (sweet pepper) and eggplant (aubergine) slices.

- **1 kg (2 lbs) fresh ricotta**
- **½ cup mixed fresh herbs (dill, sage, tarragon, thyme, parsley), roughly chopped**
- **freshly ground black pepper**
- **12 sorrel leaves**
- **olive oil to grease the loaf tin**

Preheat oven to 160°C (325°F). Brush a loaf tin sparingly with olive oil.

Combine ricotta and herbs in a bowl. Add pepper to taste, and mix gently with a fork.

Drop sorrel leaves into boiling water for a few seconds, drain immediately and refresh in cold water. Drain on a clean tea towel.

Line the loaf tin with the sorrel, draping the leaves over the edge. Spoon in ricotta mixture and fold overhanging leaves to cover top.

Bake for 45 minutes.

Cool in tin for 10 minutes, turn out onto a serving plate, and slice.

SESAME CHEESE PIE

SERVES 6

Serve hot with a crisp green salad.

- **500 g (1 lb) ricotta cheese**
- **300 ml (10 fl oz) sour cream**
- **3 eggs**
- **100 g (3½ oz) cheddar cheese, grated**
- **½ bunch green onions (green shallots or scallions), chopped**
- **3 tablespoons chopped fresh mint**
- **1 bunch chives, snipped**
- **375 g (12 oz) shortcrust or puff pastry**
- **2 tablespoons sesame seeds, for decoration**

Preheat the oven to 190°C (375°F).

Crumble ricotta into a large bowl. Beat in sour cream and two of the eggs. Stir through cheddar, green onions, mint and chives.

Cut pastry in half and roll out one half on a lightly floured surface to form a rectangle 18 cm x 33 cm (7 in x 13 in). Set on a greased baking tray.

Spoon filling over the pastry, leaving a border of 3 cm (1 in). Brush edges with water.

Roll out remaining pastry to a rectangle slightly larger than the first, and cover filling. Press the edges together to seal.

Roll edge and score with the back of a knife. Make a few slits in the top to allow steam to escape.

Beat the remaining egg and brush the pie with it. Sprinkle pie with sesame seeds.

Bake for 25 to 35 minutes, or until golden brown.

SAGE

Sage leaves have a strong, spicy, pungent flavour. They are traditionally used as an accompaniment to rich meats like pork or goose, and as a stuffing (with onion) for duckling. Sage is also much used as a flavouring for cheese and cheese dishes. It has a strong flavour, and is a herb well worth experimenting with. For instance, try using it in a sauce for sausages, or with baked tomatoes, or place a few leaves on top of grilled fish or between cubes of meat on kebabs. It's especially delicious with grilled ham. Used sparingly, sage is tasty in tossed salads and fruit cups. A marvellously aromatic honey can be made simply by steeping a few sage leaves. Sage is a delicious addition to a sharp and tangy apple jelly for serving with roast meats.

RISOTTO WITH HERBS

SERVES 4

4 cups (1 litre/32 fl oz) vegetable stock (recipe, page 14)

2 cups (500 ml/16 fl oz) dry white wine

60 g (2 oz) butter

1 small Spanish onion, chopped

350 g (11½ oz) arborio rice (short-grained white Italian rice)

¾ to 1 cup finely chopped fresh herbs (rosemary, sage, parsley, basil, oregano, marjoram, thyme, fennel)

2 cloves garlic, crushed

½ cup pine nuts, toasted (see note)

60 g (2 oz) freshly grated Parmesan cheese

salt and freshly ground black pepper

Combine stock and wine in a saucepan and heat until simmering. Reduce heat to just maintain a simmer.

Melt half the butter in a large, heavy pan or casserole. Add onion and fry lightly over a medium heat.

Add rice, stir with a wooden spoon to coat with butter.

When rice begins to stick to the pan, add a ladleful of stock mixture. Stir constantly until all the liquid is absorbed, then add another ladleful.

When half the liquid is used, add herbs, garlic and pine nuts. Continue adding liquid and cooking, until almost all the liquid is absorbed and the rice is cooked.

Stop stirring, remove from heat, and stand until the last liquid is absorbed.

Add Parmesan and remaining butter, salt and pepper to taste, and serve immediately.

Note: To toast pine nuts, spread nuts onto a shallow dish and microwave on high for 2 minutes, or bake in a hot (200°C/400°F) for 5 minutes, stirring once.

CAULIFLOWER IN YOGHURT

SERVES 6 TO 8

3 onions, finely sliced

2 cloves garlic, crushed

1 teaspoon grated fresh ginger

1 teaspoon sugar

1 cup (250 ml/8 fl oz) plain yoghurt

1 large cauliflower, broken into florets

45 g (1½ oz) ghee

⅔ cup (160 ml/5 fl oz) hot water

1 teaspoon garam masala

Combine one onion in a blender or food processor with garlic, ginger, sugar and yoghurt. Blend until smooth.

Combine cauliflower with the yoghurt mixture, and stand for at least 2 hours.

Melt ghee in saucepan, then sauté remaining onions until golden brown.

Add cauliflower mixture and hot water. Cover, and simmer over a low heat for 15 minutes, or until cauliflower is tender. Stir in garam masala.

HERBED SAFFRON CANNELLONI WITH RICOTTA AND SORREL

SERVES 4 AS A MAIN COURSE OR 6 TO 8 AS AN ENTREE

PASTA

2 cups (250 g/8 oz) unbleached bread flour

½ teaspoon saffron powder

3 to 4 eggs

¼ cup chervil leaves

2 tablespoons snipped chives

2 tablespoons olive oil

FILLING

600 g (1 lb 3½ oz) fresh ricotta

3 eggs

1 small bunch of sorrel (about 40 g/½ oz), leaves sliced

salt and freshly ground black pepper

SAUCE

60 g (2 oz) butter, and extra for greasing the baking dish

½ cup (60 g/2 oz) unbleached bread flour

1½ cups (375 ml/12 fl oz) milk

salt and pepper to taste

200 g (6½ oz) freshly grated Parmesan cheese

TO MAKE THE PASTA

Sieve flour and saffron to make a mound on the work surface. Make a well in the centre. Break 3 of the eggs into the well. Using the tip of a long metal spatula, break up the eggs, and mix a little flour into them. Then, using the long edge of

HERBED SAFFRON CANNELLONI WITH RICOTTA AND SORREL
('Wave' table and chair from Potter Williams. Pillivuyt plates from Hale Imports. Napkins from Les Olivades. Emile Henry baking dish and Bogart serving spoon and fork from The Bay Tree)

the spatula, bring the flour from the outer edge of the pile into the well, mixing as you go. Continue until all the flour is dampened.

If mixture seems very dry, break the remaining egg into it.

Knead lightly to form a ball. Roll in pasta machine, or with a long rolling-pin, until the thickness of lasagne (about 2 mm/¹⁄₁₂ in).

Cut pasta into two equal sized pieces. Scatter chervil and chives over one piece and place remaining piece on top. Press gently together. Roll again 2 to 3 times, until pieces are blended. Cut into 15 cm (6 in) lengths (or squares, if using a rolling-pin), and place in a single layer on a lightly floured board to dry.

Bring a large pot of water to a boil. Add salt to taste. Next to the pot, place a large bowl of cold water with 2 tablespoons oil. Drop each square of pasta into boiling water and cook individually, for about 5 seconds, from the time when the water returns to the boil. Lift out with a slotted spoon, and drop into the bowl of cold water.

Spread a damp tea towel onto work surface and place pasta squares on it in a single layer. If required, top with another tea towel and lay more pasta on this. Stand for 20 minutes while preparing the filling and preheating the oven to 190°C (375°F).

TO MAKE THE FILLING

Beat ricotta with eggs until light and fluffy. Stir in sorrel and salt and pepper.

Butter a baking dish.

To fill cannelloni, place each piece of pasta on a smooth surface. Spread about 3 tablespoons of the filling along one edge. Roll into a tube, starting from the edge containing the filling, and rolling towards the opposite edge. With this outer edge on the top, place the tube in the buttered baking dish.

TO MAKE THE SAUCE

Melt butter in a saucepan. Stir in flour and cook 1 minute, then gradually whisk in milk. Cook for 3 to 4 minutes, stirring, until sauce has thickened. Add salt and pepper to taste, then stir in half the Parmesan.

Pour sauce over cannelloni and sprinkle with remaining cheese.

Bake for 20 minutes. Brown cheese under grill, then stand for 10 minutes before serving.

SORREL

Sorrel has quite a refreshing, almost lemony flavour. The young leaves can be steamed or parboiled like spinach or put into soup and stews. It is good with pasta, and in potato salad. Sorrel is a traditional 'bean herb', helping to offset any 'heaviness' in dishes based around lentils or haricot beans.

WILD MUSHROOM TART

SERVES 6

1½ cups (135 g/7½ oz) unbleached wholemeal plain flour

1 teaspoon salt

125 g (4 oz) cold unsalted butter, cut into cubes

3 tablespoons lemon juice

FILLING

¼ cup (60 ml/2 fl oz) mustard seed oil

2 golden shallots (French shallots or eschalots), finely chopped

1 tablespoon mustard seeds

salt and freshly ground black pepper

250 g (8 oz) mixed fresh wild mushrooms (shiitake, enoki, porcini, pine), wiped clean, and sliced if required

250 g (8 oz) field mushrooms, wiped, and sliced

¼ cup (60 ml/2 fl oz) veal glacé (see note), or 1 cup (250 ml/ 8 fl oz) good-quality stock, reduced to ¼ cup

½ cup sliced fresh sorrel leaves

2 tablespoons lemon thyme leaves

5 eggs

200 ml (6 fl oz) crème fraîche

180 g (6 oz) shredded mozzarella cheese

125 g (4 oz) grated Parmesan cheese

TO MAKE THE PASTRY

Combine flour, salt and butter in a large bowl. Rub in butter until the mixture resembles fine breadcrumbs.

Stir in lemon to form a firm dough. Shape into a ball, wrap in plastic, and refrigerate for 1 hour.

Preheat oven to 190°C (375°F).

Roll pastry on a lightly floured surface to a thickness of 3 mm (⅛ in). Line a 23 cm (9 in) tart pan, and trim edges. Refrigerate 15 minutes.

Remove shell from refrigerator, line with baking paper, and fill with rice or baking weights. Bake for 20 minutes.

Remove tart shell from oven (do not turn off the oven). Remove rice and paper. Set shell aside to cool.

TO MAKE THE FILLING

Heat oil in a heavy frying pan. Add shallots and mustard seeds and cook, stirring, until seeds begin to pop.

Add mushrooms, and cook over a moderately high heat, stirring, for 5 minutes. Add veal glacé and cook a further 5 minutes. Seaon with salt and pepper to taste.

Remove from heat and stir in the herbs.

Beat eggs and crème fraîche together. Stir in mozzarella and Parmesan. Combine with the mustard mixture and pour into the prepared shell. Bake at 190°C (375°F) for 30 minutes.

Remove from oven and cool for 5 minutes, then cut into wedges and serve immediately.

Note: Veal glacé is a very reduced veal stock, and can be bought from good delicatessans. The alternative (good-quality stock) is just as suitable, although not quite as flavoursome.

WILD MUSHROOM TART
(La Cucina quiche dish from Gempo. Trug basket from Swing Gifts. Napkin from Les Olivades)

THYME

With its warm pungent flavour, thyme is an essential ingredient in bouquet garni, and may be used to flavour soups, stews and casseroles, as well as being added to herb mixtures for stuffings and marinades. A little thyme is excellent in egg dishes, particularly in a simple omelette or quiche. Lemon thyme is delicious with fish or chicken. Sprigs of thyme can be added to all types of potted meats and cheeses, pâtés, pickled olives, and gherkins.

Thyme is said to grow well near other herbs of Mediterranean origin, notably lavender and rosemary; also like them, thyme is much loved by bees. During the English Wars of the Roses, a design of a sprig of thyme with a bee hovering above it became a popular embroidered motif on knights' clothing, signifying courage.

GNOCCHI WITH SPINACH SAUCE

SERVES 4 TO 6

500 g (1 lb) frozen potato gnocchi

SPINACH SAUCE

2 tablespoons olive oil

2 cloves garlic, chopped

1 onion, finely chopped

1 bunch English spinach, washed, roots removed and leaves and stalks roughly chopped

½ cup chopped fresh herbs (chervil, thyme, oregano, basil)

1½ cups (375 ml/12 fl oz) beef stock (recipe, page 14)

300 ml (10 fl oz) cream

1 cup grated Parmesan cheese

salt and freshly ground black pepper

While making this recipe, bear in mind that the gnocchi and the spinach sauce need to be ready at the same time. The sauce takes 15 minutes to prepare.

TO COOK THE GNOCCHI

Consult the directions on the packet of frozen gnocchi for its cooking time, and bring a large pot of water to the boil, ready to cook the gnocchi. The gnocchi will be cooked when pieces rise to the surface.

TO MAKE THE SAUCE

Heat olive oil in a deep frying pan. Add garlic and onion, and cook over a gentle heat for five minutes. Do not brown.

Add spinach and herbs and stir to combine with onion and garlic. Add stock, and cook for five minutes.

Add cream. Simmer for five minutes.

Stir in half the Parmesan, and add salt and freshly ground black pepper to taste.

Drain the gnocchi and serve immediately with the sauce. Sprinkle with remaining Parmesan.

CHITCHKEE

SERVES 4

This dish is a mild to medium vegetable curry.

500 g (1 lb) mixed raw vegetables (see note)

2 tablespoons ghee

1 onion, sliced

2 cloves garlic, sliced

2 to 4 tablespoons curry powder

250 g (8 oz) tomatoes, peeled and chopped

1 cup (250 ml/8 fl oz) water

lemon juice, optional

Cut vegetables into even, bite size pieces.

Melt ghee in a saucepan, then sauté onion, garlic and curry powder until onion is tender.

Add tomatoes, water and vegetables, and bring to the boil. Cover, reduce heat to low, and simmer for 15 minutes or until vegetables are tender. Add a squeeze of lemon juice, if desired.

Note: These vegetables could include some or all of the following: beans, carrots, cauliflower, peas, potatoes, turnip.

SPINACH AND POTATO CURRY

SERVES 6 TO 8

- 60 g (2 oz) ghee
- 1 large onion, sliced
- 250 g (8 oz) potatoes, quartered
- 1 teaspoon ground cumin
- 2 green chillies (chili peppers), seeded and finely chopped
- ½ teaspoon ground ginger
- ½ cup (250 ml/8 fl oz) water
- 1 kg (2 lb) spinach leaves, roughly chopped

Melt ghee in saucepan, then sauté onion until tender.

Add potatoes, cumin, chillies, ginger and water. Cover, and cook over a low heat for 5 minutes, stirring occasionally.

Add spinach, cover, and cook for 2 minutes. Uncover pan, and simmer until water has evaporated. Replace lid, and cook over a very low heat for 20 minutes, or until potato is tender.

CABBAGE AND CARROT BHUJIA

SERVES 4 TO 6

- 4 tablespoons oil
- 1 tablespoon whole black mustard seeds
- 1 dried red chilli (chili pepper)
- 1 cabbage, finely sliced
- 350 g (11 oz) carrots, coarsely grated
- 1 fresh green chilli (chili pepper), cut into thin strips and seeds removed
- ½ teaspoon sugar
- 4 tablespoons chopped, fresh coriander
- 1 tablespoon lemon juice

Heat oil in a frying pan. Sauté mustard seeds and dried red chilli for one minute.

Add cabbage, carrots and green chilli. Reduce heat to low. Stir-fry the vegetables for about 30 seconds.

Add sugar and coriander. Stir-fry for another 5 minutes, or until vegetables are tender.

Add lemon juice. Remove red chilli before serving.

HERB BUTTERS

The possible combinations for herbed butters are endless. Add your selection to the basic recipe, either omitting or keeping the parsley.

BASIC RECIPE

- 125 g (4 oz) unsalted butter, at room temperature
- 1 tablespoon lemon juice
- 2 tablespoons finely chopped parsley
- salt and freshly ground black pepper

Cream butter in a small bowl, using a wooden spoon. Gradually beat in the lemon juice and parsley. Add salt and pepper to taste.

Spoon onto a piece of foil or plastic wrap and shape into a log. Wrap and refrigerate until required, for up to 2 weeks (or freeze for up to 3 months).

GARLIC BUTTER

Add 2 cloves of crushed garlic and 1 teaspoon sea salt to the basic recipe.

CHIVE BUTTER

Add chives instead of parsley to the basic recipe.

ROSEMARY BUTTER

Crush 1 tablespoon of rosemary leaves, and add to basic recipe instead of parsley.

BUTTER WITH FINES HERBES

Add the classic combination of chervil, chives, parsley and tarragon, in equal proportions.

CHIVES

Chives have a delicate onion-like flavour and may be used to add a sweetish and subtle flavour to egg dishes, salads and soups. Use them when you want just a touch of flavour, where a full strength onion would be overpowering—mix snipped chives in with cream or cottage cheese, for instance, or use as a topping. Where would we be without baked potatoes, complete with a dollop of sour cream or natural yoghurt and liberally sprinkled with chopped chives and freshly ground black pepper? Delicious!

Chives, along with shallots and leeks and garlic, belong to the onion family; in fact, an old country name for chives is 'The Little Brothers of the Onion'.

Main Meats and Sauces

Tagine of Beef with Potatoes

Blue-eye Cod and Vegetable Bake

Slow-roasted Leg of Lamb

Roast Pork Fillet Salad with Vietnamese Mint and Lime

Steak and Kidney Pie with Savoury Herbed Puff Pastry

Herbed Kangaroo Loin Fillets

Osso Buco

Chicken Breasts with Tarragon and Verjuice

Poached Ocean Trout Fillets with Green Mayonnaise

Racks of Lamb with Parsley Mint Crust

Almond Fried Chicken with Spiced Ginger Sauce

Cornfed Chicken with Herb Butter

Prawns in Herbed Coconut Milk

Tomato Sauce

Watercress Sauce

Horseradish Cream

Coriander Sauce

Dill and Yoghurt Dressing

Balsamic Vinaigrette

Rosemary Vinaigrette

Herbed Mustard Vinaigrette

Pesto

Sage and Walnut Paste

Pesto Tapenade

Coriander Pesto

SLOW-ROASTED LEG OF LAMB, PAGE 65

(Napkin from Les Olivades. Pillivuyt plates from Hale Imports)

61

TAGINE OF BEEF WITH POTATOES

SERVES 6

1.5 kg (3 lb) topside of beef, cut into 3.5 cm (1½ in) cubes

2 large Spanish onions, peeled and grated

2 tablespoons olive oil

1 teaspoon salt

1 teaspoon powdered cinnamon

1 teaspoon powdered saffron

freshly ground black pepper

¼ teaspoon powdered ginger

125 g (4 oz) butter

2 cups (500 ml/16 fl oz) beef stock (recipe, page 14)

6 medium potatoes, peeled and quartered

250 g (8 oz) dried prunes

1 strip lemon peel

2 cinnamon sticks

200 g (7 oz) blanched almonds

sea salt

½ cup roughly chopped mint, plus a handful of leaves

½ bunch watercress

Combine meat with onion, olive oil, salt, cinnamon, saffron, black pepper and ginger in a large flame-proof casserole or Dutch oven. Stir to combine well, then stand at room temperature for 2 hours or refrigerate overnight.

Add 90 g (3 oz) of the butter, the stock and enough water to just cover meat. Cook, partially covered, over a low to medium heat for 35 to 40 minutes.

Meanwhile, place prunes in a small bowl and cover with boiling water. Stand for 20 minutes, then drain.

Preheat oven to 200°C (400°F).

When cooking time for the meat is up, remove about 2 cups of cooking liquid from the pot and place in a saucepan, with drained prunes, lemon peel and cinnamon. Cook gently for 15 minutes, or until prunes are swollen and soft. Cover and set aside.

Meanwhile, add potatoes to meat in pot, cover and cook over a low heat for 15 to 20 minutes, or until tender.

Place almonds on an oven tray. Melt the remaining butter and combine with almonds. Sprinkle with sea salt. Roast in oven until golden. Reserve.

Using a slotted spoon, transfer meat and potatoes to a warm, deep serving platter. Sprinkle with chopped mint then pour over prunes and sauce (they will be warm enough). Cover with foil.

Boil meat sauce vigorously to reduce by a third, then pour over meat in serving plate. Sprinkle almonds over, and garnish plate with mint leaves and watercress.

MINT

Mint is named after the beautiful nymph Menthe, beloved of Pluto, who was changed into the sweet-scented herb by Pluto's jealous wife, Proserpine.

TAGINE OF BEEF WITH POTATOES
(Tagine dish from Accoutrement)

BLUE-EYE COD AND VEGETABLE BAKE

SERVES 4

4 Pontiac potatoes, washed, and thickly sliced

¼ cup (60 ml/2 fl oz) olive oil

1 clove garlic, crushed

salt and freshly ground black pepper

4 blue-eye cod steaks, each 2.5 cm (1 in) thick

finely pared rind and juice of 1 lemon

1 teaspoon thyme leaves, and extra sprigs for garnish

1 tablespoon chopped chervil

8 egg tomatoes, halved lengthways

1 Spanish onion, cut into wedges

1 red capsicum (sweet pepper), cut into large dice

12 black olives

Preheat oven to 190°C (375°F).

Steam potatoes for 10 minutes, or until just tender. Remove from heat and turn onto a clean disposable cloth.

Brush a large baking dish with some of the oil and spread potatoes on base in one layer. Sprinkle garlic over, then sprinkle with salt and pepper. Lay fish steaks on top, add lemon rind, and sprinkle with lemon juice. Add thyme leaves, chervil, tomatoes, onion, capsicum, and olives.

Bake for 20 minutes, or until fish is cooked.

Serve immediately, garnished with thyme sprigs.

SLOW-ROASTED LEG OF LAMB

SERVES 4

Serve with Minted Spinach Couscous (page 43) or steamed new potatoes.

1.5 kg (3 lb) leg of lamb

3 cloves garlic, slivered

6 fresh sprigs rosemary

4 Spanish onions, peeled and quartered

6 fresh sage leaves

1 tablespoon olive oil

salt and freshly ground black pepper

2 cans (each 400 g/13 oz) tomatoes

1 tablespoon fresh thyme

1 tablespoon fresh oregano

1 tablespoon honey

Preheat oven to 120°C (250°F).

Make small incisions all over top surface of lamb. Poke in slivers of garlic and sprigs of rosemary.

Place onion in a deep baking dish, sprinkle with torn sage leaves then place lamb on top and brush it with oil. Sprinkle with salt and freshly ground black pepper, cover, and bake for 4 hours.

Remove baking dish from oven. Spread honey over lamb, add undrained tomatoes, thyme and oregano, and return baking dish to oven. Increase temperature to 200°C (400°F), and cook a further 10 minutes, until lamb is golden (alternatively, brown lamb under oven grill).

Remove baking dish from oven and carefully remove the lamb (it will fall apart easily).

Slice meat onto warmed plates, and serve with the roasted tomato and onion.

ROSEMARY

Rosemary also marries well with fruit and sweets; add it to jellies, poached pears and custards. Steep a sprig in honey and use the flavoured honey when baking.

The flowers can be crystallized and used as a garnish; the dried leaves can be crumbled and added to batter for bread or a cheese scone mix.

Try rosemary as as a deliciously different flavouring in certain vegetable side dishes, notably peas and spinach. Rosemary vinegar will add zest to a plain salad.

BLUE-EYE COD AND VEGETABLE BAKE
(Photographed at Milkwood. Napkin from Les Olivades)

ROAST PORK FILLET SALAD WITH VIETNAMESE MINT AND LIME

SERVES 4 TO 6

- **750 g (1½ lb) pork fillets**

- **1 tablespoon Oriental sesame oil, and extra for sprinkling**

- **⅓ cup (80 ml/2½ fl oz) lime juice**

- **3 fresh red chillies (chili peppers), chopped**

- **1 teaspoon sugar**

- **1 clove garlic, crushed**

- **2 tablespoons fish sauce (see note, page 16)**

- **250 g (8 oz) bean sprouts**

- **1 small Spanish onion, finely sliced**

- **250 g (8 oz) snow peas (mangetout), trimmed, halved diagonally, and blanched (see note)**

- **1 bunch asparagus, trimmed and blanched (see note)**

- **¼ cup chopped fresh Vietnamese mint**

- **4 green onions (green shallots or scallions), diagonally sliced**

Preheat oven to 220°C (425°F).

Rub fillets with sesame oil. Heat a cast-iron grill pan until smoking (or heavy frying pan), add fillets, and cook 1 minute each side.

Transfer fillets, still on grill pan, to oven (or transfer to shallow baking dish) for 7 to 8 minutes.

Remove from oven and stand at room temperature, to cool slightly.

Slice pork thinly on the diagonal. Place in a shallow dish with meat juices. Combine lime juice, chilli, sugar, garlic and fish sauce, and pour over warm meat. Stand at room temperature until required.

Combine sprouts, onion, snow peas, Vietnamese mint and green onion. Arrange on a platter and top with pork and dressing. Sprinkle with a little extra sesame oil.

Note: To blanch snow peas and asparagus, drop into a large pan of boiling water, remove as soon as water returns to a boil, then immerse in a sink of cold water. Alternatively, place into a plastic bag and microwave on high for 2 minutes (peas) and 3 minutes (asparagus), then refresh in cold water immediately.

ROAST PORK FILLET SALAD WITH VIETNAMESE MINT AND LIME

(French yellow dinner plates, green glass tumblers, white Primo square platter, white damask napkins, Elegance serving fork and spoon from **The Bay Tree**)

STEAK AND KIDNEY PIE WITH SAVOURY HERBED PUFF PASTRY

SERVES 4 TO 6

I portion (500 g/I lb) savoury herbed puff pastry (recipe, page 41)

750 g (1½ lb) gravy beef, in one piece

250 g (8 oz) ox kidney

salt and freshly ground black pepper

I tablespoon plain flour

I golden shallot (French shallot or eschalot), finely chopped

I tablespoon chopped parsley

I sprig fresh thyme

2 fresh bay leaves

3 medium potatoes, peeled and quartered

2 cups (500 ml/16 fl oz) beef stock (recipe, page 14)

I egg yolk

Trim the beef and cut into 2.5 cm (1 in) cubes. Skin and core kidney and cut into 12 mm (½ in) pieces.

Combine salt, pepper and flour in a large plastic or oven bag, and add meat. Holding bag closed, toss meat around until coated with flour.

Combine shallot, herbs and potatoes, and place with meat in a 25 cm (10 in) pie dish. Pour 300 ml (½ pint) of the stock into the dish.

Preheat oven to 220°C (425°F).

Roll pastry to a thickness of 6 mm (¼ in). Cut a piece slightly larger than dish.

Re-roll the pastry scraps so they are slightly thinner, and cut two strips, each 2.5 cm (1 in) wide.

Dampen edge of pie dish with stock. Press pastry strips around edge and brush with stock.

Carefully lift the cut pastry sheet onto pie. Trim edge with scissors or a sharp knife (see note).

Re-roll any remaining scraps and cut into decorative shapes for the top of the pie.

Beat egg yolk with a pinch of salt and brush top of pastry with this.

Bake for 30 minutes, then cover pie with a sheet of foil. Reduce temperature to 160°C (325°F), and cook for another 1½ hours.

Heat remaining stock. When first slice of pie is cut, pour hot stock into pie dish to dilute the pie gravy.

Note: When trimming pastry edges, use short brisk strokes to avoid dragging the pastry (dragging will hamper the puffing process).

HERBED KANGAROO LOIN FILLETTS

SERVES 6

This recipe is equally successful with venison or pork fillets. Serve it with Oven-baked Desiree Potatoes (recipe, page 39) and Roasted Capsicums and Spanish Onions (recipe, page 35).

I kg (2 lb) kangaroo loin fillets

I bunch oregano (about 25 g/ I oz)

I bunch marjoram (about 10 g/ ½ oz)

100 g (3½ oz) sundried tomatoes, chopped

½ cup (125 ml/4 fl oz) oil from the tomatoes

freshly ground black pepper

¼ cup (60 ml/2 fl oz) walnut oil

Place meat in a flat dish with the other ingredients. Turn to coat well with the mixture. Cover and marinate for at least 2 hours (at room temperature) or overnight (refrigerated). Turn occasionally.

Bring meat to room temperature before cooking.

Preheat oven to 220°C (425°F). Heat a cast-iron grill pan on top of stove until smoking. Cook meat for 2 minutes on each side. Scrape residue of marinade over meat and place, still on grill pan, into oven for 5 minutes.

Remove from oven and stand 5 to 10 minutes, covered with foil, before cutting.

Serve cut into diagonal slices, with pan juices poured over.

> ## BAY
>
> Bay leaves can be harvested year-round and used fresh or dried. They can be added to soups, pasta dishes, casseroles, vegetables (baked potatoes are delicious when cooked with a few bay leaves), and even milk-based dishes, such as blancmange and rice pudding. The dried leaves are sweeter and less pungent to use than the fresh ones. Traditionally, a bay leaf is pressed into pâtés and home-made potted meats.

OSSO BUCO

SERVES 4

1 kg (2 lb) veal knuckle, cut in 12 mm (½ in) thick pieces

salt and pepper

flour for dusting

3 tablespoons olive oil

2 onions, chopped

¾ cup (180 ml/6 fl oz) white wine

1 can (400 g/13 oz) tomatoes, chopped, and juice

1 cup (250 ml/8 fl oz) beef stock (recipe, page 14)

1 garlic clove, crushed

1 fresh bouquet garni (see below)

juice and finely grated rind of 1 lemon

¼ cup chopped parsley

Preheat oven to 200°C (400°F).

Season veal pieces with salt and pepper, and dust with flour.

Heat oil in a large, heavy based casserole dish and brown meat in batches.

Return meat to dish, add onion, and cook 5 minutes.

Add wine, and cook over high heat until reduced by half.

Add tomatoes, stock, garlic and bouquet garni. Cover and cook in oven for 1½ hours.

Transfer meat to a deep serving dish.

Place the casserole dish over a high heat to reduce the sauce.

Remove the bouquet garni. Pour sauce over meat, and sprinkle with the lemon juice, rind, and parsley.

BOUQUET GARNI

Take 2 bay leaves, 1 sprig thyme, 3 sprigs parsley, 1 sprig rosemary, tie together with string, or wrap in a piece of muslin.

CHICKEN BREASTS WITH TARRAGON AND VERJUICE

SERVES 4

Serve accompanied by a green salad and Potato and Parmesan Tart (recipe, page 42).

4 chicken breast fillets

salt and freshly ground pink pepper

125 g (4 oz) butter

1 red onion, finely diced

2 tablespoons chopped tarragon

⅓ cup (80 ml/2½ fl oz) verjuice (see note), or white wine vinegar

Trim chicken of any fat and season with salt and pepper.

Melt half the butter in a heavy frying pan, add chicken and cook over a moderately hot heat for 3 to 5 minutes, until browned on all sides.

Cover, reduce heat to low, and cook chicken for 10 to 12 minutes, until just cooked through.

Transfer chicken to a warm dish, cover, and keep warm while making the sauce.

Add onion and tarragon to pan juices and cook over a moderate heat, stirring, until onion is soft.

Increase temperature and add verjuice, cooking until reduced to a slightly syrupy sauce. Remove pan from the heat and stir in remaining butter.

Slice chicken thinly on the diagonal and serve with sauce poured over.

Note: Verjuice is the unfermented juice of white grapes.

ROSEMARY

On rosemary: 'I lett it runne all over my garden walls, not onlie because my bees love it, but because it is the herb sacred to remembrance and, therefore, to friendship.'

—Sir Thomas More (1478-1535)

TARRAGON

French tarragon is a traditional and distinctive flavouring for many famous French dishes and sauces, notably Tartare, Bearnaise and Hollandaise.

French tarragon is marvellous in salads, heightening the flavour of other herbs and all green vegetables, especially corn, carrots and cucumbers. Eggs and fish go well with tarragon; chicken and tarragon is another classic combination. Chopped tarragon leaves can be added to shellfish dishes, meat stuffings and soups, or mixed in with herb butters.

POACHED OCEAN TROUT FILLETS WITH GREEN MAYONNAISE

SERVES 6

Serve with wedges of Pan-fried Potato Cake (recipe, page 33).

GREEN MAYONNAISE

2 egg yolks

I teaspoon mustard powder (oriental hot mustard is very good)

pinch of salt

2 teaspoons lime juice, verjuice (see note, page 69), or tarragon vinegar

300 ml (10 fl oz) extra-virgin olive oil

10 English spinach leaves

leaves from 10 sprigs watercress

leaves from 4 stems tarragon

leaves from 4 stalks parsley

FISH

2 kg (4 lb) ocean trout fillets, to give 6 servings

2 limes (I juiced and its rind finely grated, I sliced very thinly for garnish)

I stalk lemon grass, crushed

2 kaffir lime leaves

6 white peppercorns

LEMON GRASS

Lemon grass tea is believed to increase psychic powers and encourage clarity of thought.

TO MAKE THE MAYONNAISE

Whisk yolks with mustard and a pinch salt until smooth. Whisk in 1 teaspoon of the lime juice, then slowly whisk in oil, until all is incorporated and the mixture is thick and smooth. Whisk in the remaining teaspoon of lime juice.

Drop spinach, watercress, tarragon and parsley into a pan of boiling water, then immediately drain and squeeze out as much moisture as possible. Purée in a blender. Mix this into the prepared mayonnaise.

TO PREPARE THE FISH

Trim fish fillets, and use tweezers to remove any obvious bones.

Place fillets in a poaching pan or deep frying pan with the lime juice, rind, lemon grass, lime leaves and peppercorns; add cold water to just cover, and bring to a simmer over a medium heat. Cook for 2 minutes, then remove pan from heat.

Using a slotted spoon, remove fillets from the pan.

Serve at room temperature with green mayonnaise and garnished with extra lime.

POACHED OCEAN TROUT FILLETS WITH GREEN MAYONNAISE, AND CHICORY SALAD WITH SUMMER SAVORY DRESSING, PAGE 30 (Pillivuyt plate from Hale Imports. Napkin from The Bay Tree)

RACKS OF LAMB WITH PARSLEY MINT CRUST

SERVES 6

60 g (2 oz) butter

1 tablespoon mango chutney

2 teaspoons French mustard

1 clove garlic, crushed

2 teaspoons lemon juice

6 racks lamb (4 chops each), trimmed of excess fat

6 tablespoons finely chopped fresh parsley

2 tablespoons finely chopped fresh mint

salt and freshly ground black pepper

2 mangoes, peeled, seeded and sliced

MANGO MINT SAUCE

1 mango, peeled, seeded and puréed

1 tablespoon finely chopped fresh mint

freshly ground black pepper

1 teaspoon vinegar

Preheat oven to 200°C (400°F).

Combine butter, chutney, mustard, garlic and lemon juice. Spread evenly over the back of each lamb chop. Sprinkle over parsley and mint, and press onto lamb using the back of a metal spoon. Season well with salt and pepper. Cook in oven for 20 to 30 minutes, or until tender.

To make sauce, combine ingredients in a small saucepan. Heat gently, then serve.

ALMOND FRIED CHICKEN WITH SPICED GINGER SAUCE

SERVES 6

This dish can be served hot or cold.

2 kg (4 lb) chicken pieces

¼ cup (30 g/1 oz) ground almonds

⅓ cup (20 g/⅓ oz) dried breadcrumbs

⅔ cup (80 g/2½ oz) grated Parmesan cheese

salt and freshly ground black pepper

2 eggs

1 tablespoon milk

⅓ cup (40 g/1½ oz) plain flour

oil, for frying

SPICED GINGER SAUCE

1 tablespoon finely grated ginger root

1 teaspoon whole allspice

1 teaspoon whole peppercorns

½ teaspoon mustard seeds

½ teaspoon whole cloves

⅔ cup (160 ml/5 fl oz) dry white wine

3 tablespoons white wine vinegar

2 tablespoons soy sauce

Remove skin from chicken pieces. Pat chicken dry with a paper towel.

Combine almonds, breadcrumbs, Parmesan, salt and pepper. Set aside.

In another bowl, blend together eggs and milk.

Dip chicken pieces in flour, then in egg mixture, and then in almond mixture.

Heat oil in frying pan. Fry chicken portions gently for 10 minutes, turning to brown all sides. Drain on paper towel.

To make the sauce, combine ginger and spices in a mortar and pestle and crush lightly. (If you do not have a mortar and pestle, place ginger and spices on a sheet of aluminium foil and crush with a rolling pin.)

Combine white wine, vinegar and soy sauce in a small saucepan. Add spices and gently heat until boiling. Boil for 8 minutes, then strain.

Serve sauce in a shallow bowl suitable for dipping.

MINT

Mint is traditionally used as an accompaniment to roast meat, especially lamb and duck. It often appears in Middle Eastern cookery, in sauces, chutneys and yoghurt-based dressings or sauces, and in spicy dishes such as couscous.

Mint brings out the flavour of summer vegetables, such as baby carrots, new potatoes, broad beans, and peas. It even has the property of being able to prevent milk from curdling!

To make syrup of mint: 'Take a quart of Syrup of Quinces before they are full ripe, juice of mint two quarts, an ounce of Red Roses, steep them twenty-four hours in the juices, then boil till it is half wasted, strain out the remainder and make it into a syrup with double refined sugar.'

—*The Receipt Book of John Nott, Cook to the Duke of Bolton,* 1723

CORNFED CHICKEN WITH HERB BUTTER

SERVES 4

I size 15 (1.5 kg/3 lb) cornfed chicken

salt and freshly ground black pepper

180 g (6 oz) unsalted butter, at room temperature

I cup chopped parsley

½ cup chopped chives

2 tablespoons rosemary leaves

2 tablespoons thyme leaves

2 tablespoons chopped sage

3 tablespoons olive oil

fresh herbs, to garnish

Preheat oven to 180°C (350°F).

Rinse chicken and pat dry. Sprinkle cavity with salt and pepper. Combine butter and herbs in food processor and process to a paste.

Gently ease skin away from the top of the chicken with your fingers, starting at the breast end. Spread the herb butter evenly over the bird between the skin and the meat. Smooth the skin back in place and tie bird to retain shape during cooking.

Place on a rack in a roasting dish and bake for 1 hour.

Increase heat to 190°C (375°F), and continue to cook until skin is crisp and golden, about 15 minutes more. Baste with pan juices.

Serve garnished with fresh herbs.

SAGE

For thousands of years, sage tea has been used as a refreshing drink, and as a medicinal beverage. Apart from its use as a spring tonic and an appetite stimulant, sage was believed to confer longevity:

'In short, 'tis a plant endow'd with so many and wonderful properties that the assiduous use of it is said to render men immortal.'

—John Evelyn (1620-1706)

PRAWNS IN HERBED COCONUT MILK

SERVES 6

Serve with plain boiled rice.

½ cup (125ml/4 fl oz) mustard seed oil

2 large onions, finely chopped

4 cloves garlic, finely chopped

2 tablespoons finely grated fresh ginger root

3 small green chillies (chili peppers), seeded, and chopped

½ teaspoon turmeric

2 tablespoons ground coriander

2 cans coconut milk (each 340 ml/12 oz)

I teaspoon sea salt

1.5 kg (3 lb) green king prawns (shrimps), shelled to tail, and deveined

¼ cup finely chopped coriander leaves

Heat oil in large, deep saucepan. Add onion and cook, stirring, over a high heat until golden.

Reduce heat to medium; add garlic, ginger, chilli, turmeric, and ground coriander. Stir for 30 seconds, then add coconut milk and salt.

Cook, uncovered, over a medium heat for about 10 minutes, stirring frequently. Add prawns, reduce heat to low, and simmer uncovered for 5 to 7 minutes, or until prawns are just cooked.

Mix in coriander and serve immediately.

CORIANDER

Coriander's fragrant seeds are used in garam masala and other curry seasoning mixes. Crushed seeds are used to flavour sweet and savoury foods, especially pickled onions and marinades.

Ground coriander is often used in baking biscuits and apple tarts: it gives a most unusual and spicy undertone to jams and marmalades.

In Germany, whole coriander seeds are added to festive breads. The seeds are also used to flavour liqueurs and spirits, being well known, along with juniper, as a flavouring agent for gin.

Coriander leaves are used as a garnish in much the same way as parsley, and as an ingredient in meat and rice dishes of the Vietnamese, Thai, and Spanish cuisines. The leaves are a perfect foil to chillies and garlic.

TOMATO SAUCE

**MAKES 6 CUPS
(1.5 LITRES/48 FL OZ)**

- **2 tablespoons olive oil**
- **1 cup finely chopped spring onions**
- **2 cloves garlic, chopped**
- **2.5 kg (5½ lb) ripe tomatoes, peeled, seeded, and diced**
- **⅓ cup dry red wine**
- **1 tablespoon fresh thyme leaves**
- **1 tablespoon chopped fennel**
- **1 teaspoon Tabasco**
- **1 strip lemon rind**
- **salt and freshly ground black pepper**

Heat the oil in a large, heavy based saucepan. Add spring onion and garlic and cook, stirring, until soft.

Add remaining ingredients, bring to the boil, reduce heat and partially cover. Cook sauce, stirring frequently, for about 25 minutes, or until thick.

Transfer to glass containers, and seal. Refrigerate or freeze until required.

FENNEL

Fennel's bulbous stalk, often sold as the vegetable 'aniseed', can be eaten raw in salads, or blanched and combined with other cooked vegetables such as carrots. The stems can be trimmed and steamed or boiled like asparagus, and then served as a side dish to pork or lamb.

TOMATO SAUCE

(Le Crueset casserole from J.D. Milner & Assoc.)

WATERCRESS SAUCE

MAKES 1½ CUPS (375 ML/12 FL OZ)

Serve with fish and salads, or as a dip for crudités.

- **1 bunch watercress, yellow leaves and root ends discarded**
- **3 green onions (green shallots or scallions), chopped**
- **½ cup chopped fresh dill**
- **4 anchovy fillets, drained**
- **3 cloves garlic, peeled**
- **1 tablespoon capers, drained**
- **1 tablespoon canned green peppercorns, drained**
- **½ cup (125 ml/4 fl oz) lemon juice**
- **¾ cup (180 ml/6 fl oz) olive oil**

Chop watercress roughly and place in food processor with green onion and dill. Chop finely. Add anchovies, garlic, capers, peppercorns and lemon juice. Process until smooth.

With machine running, slowly add oil until incorporated.

HORSERADISH CREAM

MAKES 1½ CUPS (375 ML/12 FL OZ)

Delicious with barbecued beef.

- **1 cup (250 ml/8 fl oz) thickened cream, whipped**
- **1 tablespoon horseradish cream**
- **1 green onion (green shallot or scallion), chopped finely**
- **1 tablespoon chopped fresh parsley**

Fold together, and serve.

Note: Bottles of prepared horseradish cream are readily available from supermarkets.

CORIANDER SAUCE

MAKES 1½ CUPS (375 ML/12 FL OZ)

Use as a dressing for pasta or potato salad, or as a sauce with seafood or chicken.

- **1 bunch fresh coriander leaves, washed thoroughly**
- **8 cloves garlic, peeled**
- **1½ tablespoons white wine vinegar**
- **1 tablespoon Dijon mustard**
- **300 ml (10 fl oz) extra-virgin olive oil**
- **salt and freshly ground black pepper**

Blend together coriander, garlic, vinegar and mustard until smooth. With machine running, slowly add oil until all is incorporated. Add salt and pepper to taste.

Transfer to a glass jar, cover, and store in a cool place until required.

DILL AND YOGHURT DRESSING

MAKES 1½ CUPS (375 ML/12 FL OZ)

- **1 cup (250 ml/8 fl oz) plain yoghurt**
- **1 tablespoon finely chopped golden shallot (French shallot or eschalot)**
- **¼ cup finely snipped fresh dill**
- **1 tablespoon tiny capers, rinsed and drained**
- **1 teaspoon celery seed**

Combine all ingredients in a bowl. Store, covered in refrigerator.

BALSAMIC VINAIGRETTE

MAKES 1½ CUPS (375 ML/12 FL OZ)

- **1 small red chilli (chili pepper), halved, seeded, and lightly crushed**
- **½ cup (125 ml/4 fl oz) balsamic vinegar**
- **½ cup (125 ml/4 fl oz) freshly squeezed orange juice, strained**
- **⅓ cup (80 ml/2½ fl oz) freshly squeezed lemon juice, strained**
- **¼ cup (60 ml/2 fl oz) light olive oil**
- **1 tablespoon chopped fresh marjoram or oregano**
- **salt and freshly ground black pepper**

Rub inside of a screw-top glass jar with chilli halves. Discard chilli. Combine remaining ingredients in jar, shake well and refrigerate until required.

ROSEMARY VINAIGRETTE

MAKES 1¼ CUPS (310 ML/10 FL OZ)

- **¼ cup (60 ml/2 fl oz) vegetable oil**
- **¼ cup (60 ml/2 fl oz) chicken stock (recipe, page 14)**
- **¼ cup (60 ml/2 fl oz) verjuice (see note, page 69), or white wine vinegar**
- **¼ cup (60 ml/2 fl oz) lemon juice**
- **2 tablespoons fresh rosemary leaves**
- **1 tablespoon Dijon mustard**
- **freshly ground black pepper**

Combine all ingredients in a screw-top jar and shake well. Chill.

HERBED MUSTARD VINAIGRETTE

MAKES 2 CUPS (500 ML/16 FL OZ)

- **⅓ cup (80 ml/2½ fl oz) tarragon vinegar**
- **⅓ cup (80 ml/2½ fl oz) Dijon mustard**
- **⅓ cup (80 ml/2½ fl oz) mustard seed oil**
- **⅔ cup (180 ml/6 fl oz) light olive oil**
- **½ cup (125 ml/4 fl oz) chopped mixed chives, tarragon, chervil**
- **salt and freshly ground black pepper**

Whisk vinegar and mustard together. Add oils gradually, whisking. Stir in remaining ingredients.

Store in a screw-top jar. Shake before using.

ROSEMARY

Rosemary also marries well with fruit and sweets; add it to jellies, poached pears and custards. Steep a sprig in honey and use the flavoured honey when baking.

The flowers can be crystallized and used as a garnish; the dried leaves can be crumbled and added to batter for bread or a cheese scone mix.

Try rosemary as as a deliciously different flavouring in certain vegetable side dishes, notably peas and spinach. Rosemary vinegar will add zest to a plain salad.

PESTO

**MAKES ABOUT 2 CUPS
(500 ML/16 FL OZ)**

Serve with pasta as a sauce, spread on bread, over chicken fillets before grilling, with fish and meat — an extremely useful summer essential!

- **1 bunch fresh basil, leaves only (about 60 g/2 oz)**
- **2 cloves garlic, peeled**
- **90 g (3 oz) pine nuts, lightly roasted (see note)**
- **½ teaspoon salt**
- **freshly ground black pepper**
- **90 g (3 oz) freshly grated Parmesan cheese**
- **1½ cups (375 ml/12 fl oz) extra-virgin olive oil**

Blend together all ingredients, except oil, until smooth. Slowly add oil, blending as you go, until incorporated and the mixture is the consistency of a sauce.

Transfer to a glass jar, pour a little more oil on the surface, and seal.

Note: To lightly roast pine nuts, spread nuts onto a shallow dish and microwave on high for 2 minutes, or bake in a hot oven (200°C/400°F) for 5 minutes, stirring once.

SAGE AND WALNUT PASTE

**MAKES ABOUT 3 CUPS
(750 ML/24 FL OZ)**

Use as a dressing for potato salad, as a spread on bread or bruschetta with white cheese, or on pasta as a dressing.

- **2 cups sage leaves**
- **2 cups walnut pieces, roasted (see note, page 34)**

- **1 teaspoon paprika**
- **1 teaspoon salt**
- **90 g (3 oz) freshly grated Parmesan or pecorino cheese**
- **1½ cups (375 ml/12 fl oz) walnut oil**

Blend together all ingredients, except oil, until smooth. Slowly add oil, blending as you go, until incorporated and the mixture is the consistency of a sauce.

Transfer to a glass jar, pour a little more oil on the surface, and seal.

PESTO TAPENADE

**MAKES ABOUT 2 CUPS
(500 ML/16 FL OZ)**

Use a spread with Bruschetta (recipe, page 26), as a sauce with pasta, grilled chicken or meat, or as a marinading paste prior to cooking.

- **1 bunch fresh basil, leaves only (about 60 g/2 oz)**
- **2 cloves garlic, peeled**
- **125 g (4 oz) marinated kalamata olives, stoned**
- **10 anchovy fillets**
- **1 tablespoon anchovy oil**
- **1 tablespoon lemon juice**
- **90 g (3 oz) freshly grated Parmesan cheese**
- **freshly ground black pepper**
- **1 cup (250 ml/8 fl oz) olive oil**

Blend together all ingredients, except oil, until smooth. Slowly add oil, blending as you go, until incorporated and the mixture is the consistency of a sauce. Transfer to a glass jar, pour a little more oil on the surface, and seal.

CORIANDER PESTO

**MAKES ABOUT 2 CUPS
(500 ML/16 FL OZ)**

This is particularly good with seafood, and as a marinade for skewered lamb fillets, to be barbecued or char-grilled. Serve extra pesto as a sauce.

- **1 bunch coriander, leaves and stalks only, washed (about 120 g/4 oz)**
- **3 cloves garlic, peeled**
- **finely grated rind and juice of 1 lime**
- **½ cup sesame seeds, roasted (see note)**
- **1 small red chilli (chili pepper), chopped**
- **½ cup Oriental sesame oil**
- **½ cup peanut oil**

Blend together all ingredients, except oils, until smooth. Slowly add combined oils, blending as you go, until incorporated and the mixture is the consistency of a sauce.

Transfer to a glass jar, pour a little more oil on the surface, and seal.

Note: To roast sesame seeds, spread seeds onto a shallow dish and microwave on high for 2 to 3 minutes, or bake in a hot oven (200°C/400°F) for 5 minutes, stirring once.

DILL

To make dill vinegar: steep a few seedheads of dill in 500 ml (16 fl oz) vinegar, strain after about 10 days, and pop in a few dill flowers if the vinegar is to be a gift.

Breads, Scones and Muffins

Herbed Muffins

Herbed Buttermilk Bread

Roti with Fennel, Garlic
and Green Chilli

Vegetable Chapattis

Stuffed Parathas

Rosemary Focaccia

Potato Scones with Rosemary, Sage
and Thyme

Dill Soda Scones

Dilled Oat Bread

Walnut Beer Bread

Olive and Herb Griddle Scones

Lavender Shortbread

HERBED MUFFINS, PAGE 80, AND HERBED BUTTERMILK BREAD, PAGE 80
(Photographed at Milkwood)

HERBED MUFFINS

MAKES 12

- I cup cooked brown rice, cooled (⅓ cup rice cooked in ⅔ cup water)
- 3 tablespoons walnut oil, and extra for oiling the muffin tins
- 2 eggs
- I cup (250 ml/8 fl oz) buttermilk
- ¼ cup grated Parmesan cheese
- I tablespoon finely chopped fresh herbs (oregano, marjoram, thyme, rosemary)
- I cup (155 g/5 oz) unbleached wholemeal flour
- I cup (125 g/4 oz) unbleached plain flour
- 4 teaspoons baking powder
- ½ teaspoon salt

Preheat oven to 210°C (425°F). Grease the muffin tins.

Combine rice, oil, eggs, milk, cheese and herbs.

Sift the dry ingredients together, then add the rice mixture, stirring as little as possible. Fill greased muffin tins three-quarters full, and bake for 15 minutes.

DILL

Dill seeds have a warming, pungent flavour and aroma, and taste rather like caraway, but stronger. They may be ground and used to flavour cakes, pies and sweets, or added whole to cooked vegetables. Adding dill seeds to the cooking water for cabbage will help mask the odour and improve the digestibility of the cabbage.

THYME

The opening summer, the sky
The shining moorland—to hear
The drowsy bee, as of old,
Hum o'er the thyme.

—Matthew Arnold (1822-88)

HERBED BUTTERMILK BREAD

MAKES ONE LOAF

- I cup (125 g/4 oz) unbleached bread flour
- I cup (125 g/4 oz) barley flour
- I teaspoon baking powder
- ½ teaspoon baking soda
- ½ teaspoon salt
- 90 g (3 oz) butter, melted, and extra for greasing the loaf tin
- 2 eggs, beaten
- I cup (250 ml/8 fl oz) buttermilk
- ⅓ cup honey
- ½ cup chopped fresh herbs (oregano, thyme, tarragon, chervil, parsley, chives)

Preheat oven to 180°C (350°F). Grease a loaf tin 12.5 cm x 23 cm (5 in x 9 in).

Sift dry ingredients into a large bowl.

Beat melted butter, eggs, buttermilk and honey until light and frothy. Stir in herbs.

Make a well in centre of dry ingredients, pour in herb mixture and mix until thoroughly combined.

Pour into the loaf tin, and bake for 40 to 50 minutes, or until a fine skewer inserted into the centre of the loaf comes out clean. Turn onto a wire rack to cool.

ROTI WITH FENNEL, GARLIC AND GREEN CHILLI

MAKES 24

Serve with raita and smoked salmon, or as an accompaniment to a curry or spicy meal.

- 3 medium potatoes, scrubbed
- 3 tablespoons light vegetable oil
- 200 g (6½ oz) barley flour
- 125 g (4 oz) unbleached bread flour, and extra for dusting
- 4 tablespoons chopped fennel leaves
- 3 small green chillies (chili peppers), seeded, and cut into fine strips
- 2 cloves garlic, finely chopped

Boil potatoes until tender, about 25 to 30 minutes. Drain, and allow potatoes to cool a little before peeling them. Mash potatoes with oil. Then, using your hands, combine with remaining ingredients in a large bowl. Work until the mixture clears the sides of the bowl and is non-sticky and kneadable. (Dough can be wrapped and refrigerated or frozen at this stage.)

Turn dough out onto a floured surface and knead for 3 minutes, until it is soft but not sticky.

Divide dough into four pieces and roll each into a 15 cm (6 in) log. Cut each log into six and shape each piece into a smooth ball.

Form each ball into a flat disc, patting out with your fingers, to a diameter of about 15 cm (6 in), dusting well with flour. Spread out on a large tray. (If keeping for any length of time before cooking, stack the discs, keeping them separate with pieces of plastic or baking paper.)

Heat a heavy based frying pan or cast-iron griddle over a high heat for 3 minutes. Reduce heat slightly, brush very lightly with oil, and place one round of dough in the pan and cook until underside is spotted brown, about 1 minute.

Remove from pan, brush with butter if desired, wrap in a clean tea towel and keep warm while cooking remainder. Brush pan very lightly with oil, if required.

The cooked roti can also be toasted over a flame or on a barbecue.

VEGETABLE CHAPATTIS

MAKES 6 TO 8

315 g (10 oz) plain flour

1 teaspoon salt

1 onion, finely sliced

1 tablespoon coriander or watercress leaves, finely chopped

½ red capsicum (sweet pepper), finely chopped

¼ cup (60 ml) oil

ice-cold water

Sieve the flour and salt together. Add onion, herbs and capsicum, and mix well.

Use sufficient water to make a soft dough.

Divide dough into walnut-sized balls. Flatten and roll out thinly.

Heat a frying pan, brush it with oil, and fry the chapattis (they should be like thick pancakes) on both sides until brown.

STUFFED PARATHAS

MAKES 4

1 cup (125 g/4 oz) plain flour, sifted

60 g (2 oz) butter

cold water

1 tablespoon horseradish cream (see note)

Rub 15 g (½ oz) of the butter into the flour and add sufficient water to make a soft dough.

Divide the dough into 8 parts. Roll out each of the eight pieces thinly into a round shape.

Spread horseradish on one round, and cover with another. Repeat to make 4 parathas.

Melt remaining butter in a frying pan, add parathas, cook on both sides until browned and cooked through.

Note: Bottles of prepared horseradish cream are readily available from supermarkets.

ROSEMARY FOCACCIA

SERVES 6

1 tablespoon compressed yeast

⅔ cup (160 ml/5 fl oz) warm water

4 cups (500 g/1 lb) unbleached bread flour

5 tablespoons olive oil

⅓ cup (80 ml/2½ fl oz) water

1 tablespoon fresh rosemary leaves, and extra sprigs for garnish

3 teaspoons sea salt

In a large bowl, dissolve yeast in the warm water, then stand for 10 minutes.

Mix in half the flour, knead for 10 minutes with the dough hook if using an electric mixer, or until dough reaches 'earlobe' texture.

Turn dough into a floured bowl, cover and stand in a warm, draught-free position until doubled in bulk—up to 3 hours.

Punch down, knead in the electric mixer for 10 minutes, adding remaining flour, 4 tablespoons of the olive oil, the rosemary leaves, and 2 teaspoons salt.

Rise again until doubled in bulk (another 3 hours). The dough at this stage may be left in the refrigerator for 12 hours or overnight, to rise slowly.

Preheat oven to 200°C (400°F).

Divide dough in half. Roll into two circles or squares, each 12 mm (½ in) thick. Place on lightly floured baking trays, brush with remaining oil, and sprinkle with remaining salt.

Bake for 25 to 30 minutes.

Serve warm or at room temperature. For a crunchier crust, heat each side of the focaccia under a hot grill for a few minutes.

VARIATION

Sprinkle surface with chopped olives, mixed dried herbs or chopped onion before baking. Add a little of your choice to the mixture, in the same way as the rosemary leaves are used in this recipe.

POTATO SCONES WITH ROSEMARY, SAGE AND THYME

MAKES 12

These scones are good eaten warm or cold, or refried and served as part of a breakfast, or as a light meal with ham or prosciutto and Roasted Tomato Relish (recipe, page 35).

750 g (1½ lb) old potatoes

salt

180 g (6 oz) plain flour, plus extra for flouring the board

1 teaspoon fresh rosemary leaves

1 teaspoon finely chopped sage leaves

1 teaspoon thyme leaves

30 g (1 oz) unsalted butter

Peel and boil the potatoes until soft when pierced with a knife. Drain and turn onto a large, lightly floured board. Crush with a potato masher or large fork, then sprinkle with salt to taste. Gradually add flour, kneading in lightly but thoroughly after each addition. Knead in herbs.

Form mixture into a disc. Roll out as thinly as possible and cut into rounds the size of a dinner plate. Cut each of these into quarters.

Heat a heavy based frying pan or griddle iron (the temperature is correct when a few drops of water sprinkled onto it dance around). Grease lightly with butter.

Cook scones over a moderately hot heat for 7 to 10 minutes, until golden brown, turning once only.

LEFT: ROTI WITH FENNEL, GARLIC AND GREEN CHILLI, PAGE 80.

BELOW: POTATO SCONES WITH ROSEMARY, SAGE AND THYME
(Blue jug from J.D. Milner & Assoc.)

DILL SODA SCONES

MAKES ABOUT 16

Serve hot with soup, or cold and spread with soft cream cheese and smoked salmon or thinly sliced smoked meats.

- **500 g (1 lb) plain flour**
- **1 teaspoon salt**
- **1 teaspoon bicarbonate of soda**
- **45 g (1½ oz) butter**
- **300 ml (10 fl oz) buttermilk**
- **2 tablespoons chopped dill**

Preheat oven to 220°C (425°F).

Sift flour with salt and bicarbonate of soda into a bowl. Rub in butter until mixture resembles fine breadcrumbs, then quickly mix in combined buttermilk and dill to form a soft dough.

Turn onto a floured board, knead lightly, then roll out to a thickness of about 2 cm (¾ in).

Stamp out 5 cm (2 in) circles or cut into triangles.

Bake on a lightly floured baking sheet for 12 to 15 minutes, until well risen and golden brown. Remove from oven and wrap in a clean tea towel placed on a wire rack.

FENNEL

Fennel seeds are delicious when used as a flavouring for milk-based puddings, blanc-manges and apple pies. Fennel seed oil is used to flavour sweets, cordials and liqueurs.

DILLED OAT BREAD

MAKES 1 LOAF

- **¼ cup (45 g/1½ oz) brown sugar**
- **½ cup (125 ml/4 fl oz) warm water**
- **2 tablespoons dried yeast**
- **1 small onion, chopped**
- **2 cups (500 g/16 oz) cottage cheese**
- **3 tablespoons butter**
- **2 teaspoons salt**
- **2 eggs**
- **2 cups (370 g/12 oz) buckwheat flour**
- **1½ cups (230 g/7½ oz) wholemeal flour**
- **1 cup (90 g/3 oz) rolled oats**
- **2 tablespoons dill seeds**

Dissolve 1 teaspoon of the sugar in water, sprinkle yeast over and leave in a warm place until frothy.

Blend together cheese, onion, butter, salt, eggs and the remaining sugar. Set aside.

Mix flour with oats and pour in yeast liquid. Stir in cheese mixture and dill seeds. Knead until smooth.

Place dough in warmed, lightly greased bowl and cover with a damp tea towel. Leave dough in a warm place until doubled in size.

Knock back dough and place in 1.5 litre (48 fl oz) casserole. Cover again and leave to double in size a second time.

Heat the oven to 180°C (350°F). Bake loaf for 35 minutes, or until cooked.

LOVAGE

Lovage leaves can be chopped finely and used to flavour soups and stews. The stalks can be peeled and chopped, and cooked and served as a vegetable side dish, perhaps with a white or tomato-based sauce. The stems can also be candied, rather like angelica. For those looking to include more vegetarian dishes in their diet, lovage is a worthwhile herb to have in the kitchen, for it can really give zing to otherwise bland dishes, either by itself or as part of a bouquet garni. Use it sparingly, though, as it is a very strong-tasting herb, suiting more robust vegetables like cabbage and potatoes rather than egg-based dishes. In Italy, lovage seeds are a traditional ingredient in savoury breads, such as focaccia. An oil distilled from the seeds is used to flavour cordials and some confectionery.

Lovage has a long and quite colourful history, being mentioned in the early writings of Europe and Asia. It is native to the Mediterranean area and, as with so many plants there, was introduced to Britain and northern Europe by the Romans before moving throughout the world.

WALNUT BEER BREAD

MAKES 2 LOAVES

- 1½ cups (375ml/12 fl oz) beer
- 2 sachets (each 7 g/¼ oz) dry yeast
- 560 g (1 lb 2 oz) unbleached plain flour
- 60 g (2 oz) rye flour
- 1 tablespoon salt
- 2 tablespoons raw sugar
- ½ cup walnut oil, and extra for coating bowl and oiling tins
- ½ cup finely chopped chives
- ¾ cup coarsely chopped walnuts
- 2 tablespoons fresh rosemary leaves
- 1 egg

Heat beer to lukewarm, and mix ½ cup (125 ml/4 fl oz) with the yeast in a small bowl. Cover and stand in a warm position for about 10 minutes, until frothy.

Sift flours and salt into a large bowl. Mix in sugar, then make a well in centre. Add yeast mixture, remaining beer, and oil. Mix until combined.

Turn on to a lightly floured surface and knead for 10 minutes (or 5 minutes in an electric mixer) until the dough is of 'earlobe' texture.

Brush a large bowl with extra walnut oil. Place dough in bowl, turning to coat with oil. Cover with a clean, damp tea towel and stand in a warm, draft-free place for 1 to 2 hours, or until doubled in bulk. (Dough also can be refrigerated overnight for a slow rise.)

Punch down, turn onto a lightly floured work surface and knead in chives and walnuts and rosemary.

Divide dough in half and shape each half into a 20 cm (8 in) log. Place in lightly oiled loaf tins, cover and stand in a warm, draft-free position for about 1 hour, or until almost doubled in bulk.

Preheat oven to 190°C (375°F).

Beat egg with 2 teaspoons water and a pinch of salt. Brush surface of loaves with this egg wash. Bake for 50 minutes, or until browned and cooked through. Cool in tins for 10 minutes, then turn out onto a wire rack.

OLIVE AND HERB GRIDDLE SCONES

MAKES 8

Serve hot, split and topped with slices of preserved Bocconcini (recipe, page 24), ricotta da tavola or farmer's cheese, sundried tomatoes and rocket.

- 250 g (8 oz) unbleached bread flour
- ¼ teaspoon salt
- 1 teaspoon bicarbonate soda
- 60 g (2 oz) butter or lard
- 1 teaspoon cream of tartar
- 150 ml (5 fl oz pint) buttermilk
- 2 tablespoons chopped black olives
- 1 teaspoon rosemary leaves
- 1 tablespoon chopped marjoram or oregano
- olive oil, for pan

Sift together flour, salt and bicarbonate of soda into a bowl. Rub in butter or lard until mixture resembles fine breadcrumbs.

Dissolve cream of tartar in the buttermilk, then stir in the olives and herbs. Quickly stir into the flour mixture to give a firm dough.

Turn onto a floured board, divide in half, and shape into two rounds, each about 12 mm (½ in) thick. Cut each round into quarters, and dust lightly with flour.

Heat a heavy frying pan or griddle iron (the temperature is correct when a few drops of water sprinkled onto it dance around). Brush lightly with olive oil.

Place one scone circle onto the pan. Cook over a moderately hot heat for 3 to 5 minutes, until underside is browned. Turn and cook the top. Repeat with remaining dough.

TARRAGON

Tarragon's early use appears to have been mainly medicinal. The Roman naturalist Pliny wrote that tarragon prevented fatigue, and even today pilgrims place sprigs in their shoes. Tarragon's Latin name, *Artemisia dracunculus*, means 'little dragon', because long ago it was thought to cure the bites of dragons and other venomous beasts.

Unlike most other herbs, the culinary use of tarragon does not appear much in literature until Tudor times, when it became enormously popular as a 'salading'. Tarragon has a distinctive aromatic and warming flavour. Very good quality French tarragon has a spicy 'bite'.

LAVENDER SHORTBREAD

MAKES ABOUT 25

ABOVE: **ROSEMARY FOCACCIA, PAGE 81**

RIGHT: **LAVENDER SHORTBREAD** (Photographed at Milkwood)

Rosemary leaves can be substituted for lavender in this recipe.

- **180 g (6 oz) unsalted butter, at room temperature**
- **125 g (4 oz) caster sugar, in which a few lavender flowers (or leaves if you prefer a stronger flavour) have been stored, at least overnight**
- **180 g (6oz) plain flour**
- **90 g (3 oz) rice flour**
- **lavender flowers for decoration**

Preheat oven to 190°C (375°F).

Beat butter until pale and smooth, then gradually beat in 90 g (3 oz) of the sifted sugar. Sift combined flours and quickly stir in to butter mixture to form a paste. Press in to a 23 cm (9 in) flan or sandwich tin. Mark slices with the back of a knife, then sprinkle remaining caster sugar over top.

Bake for 20 minutes, or until pale golden. Cool in tin. Cut into slices where marked, and decorate with a few lavender flowers.

A Guide to Growing Herbs

BASIL

In warm or temperate climates, basil may be treated as a perennial; however, if you life in a cool area, treat it as a tender annual. Plant seeds outside well after the danger of frost has passed; or, if sowing seed in early spring, keep pots indoors or in a heated greenhouse. Germination is fairly quick, taking about a week.

Basil grows best in a well drained light rich soil in a bright sunny spot. If you are planting indoors, a sun-filled kitchen windowsill is usually ideal. Thin seedlings once they are established (you could put half in the garden, and half in a pot in the kitchen for ready use), and dress with plenty of well rotted manure or compost. Keep basil well watered, as it likes plenty of moisture as well as heat. Pinch out the flower buds as the plant grows, to encourage bushiness.

When planted in the garden, basil will grow to a height of about 60 cm (24 in). It makes an excellent companion plant for tomatoes, helping to repel pests such as white fly.

Harvest by trimming the plant down to the second pair of leaves as the buds form. Use the fresh leaves, or dry and store them in airtight opaque containers.

Sweet basil is the main variety; other species worth seeking out include the decorative purple-leafed basil 'Dark Opal', the large 'Lettuce Leaf' and low-growing bush basil, along with curled leaf, lemon-scented and even liquorice- and cinnamon-scented varieties.

BAY

The evergreen sweet bay tree (also called roman laurel) can be grown from seed or from cuttings taken in midsummer. Cuttings are probably the easiest method. Take them from new growth, ensuring each has a 'heel', and dip in a propagating powder before planting into pots. If you live in a very cold area, you may need to protect your new plants in a cold frame or warm greenhouse while they become established. Within six months you should have a sapling that is suitable for planting out, either in a large tub or in a sunny sheltered spot in the garden.

A bay tree will prefer a well drained and well composted soil. It is susceptible to frost so, if your area experiences harsh winters, you are well advised to settle your bay tree in a decorative wheeled tub and trundle it inside for safekeeping during winter.

A bay tree will grow slowly; it responds well to regular light pruning and trimming—harvest the leaves regularly once the tree is established—and it thrives as a topiary specimen, clipped into a ball or cone shape. If cultivated in a pot, a bay tree usually won't exceed 2 m (6 ft); allowed to spread freely in a garden over time, they can achieve 4.5 m to 6 m (15 to 20 ft).

Bay leaves may be harvested year-round and used fresh or dried.

CHERVIL

Chervil is a small, dainty herb. Its lacy, fern-like leaves are a light bright green when young, and a soft dark pink when mature. Chervil is an annual, growing to a height of 30 cm to 45 cm (12 in to 18 in).

Seed can be planted in spring. As it self-sows readily, your problem may well be how to hold it back! Water seeds well and keep the tiny plants sheltered from wind and frost before planting out, as the fine foliage dries out rapidly.

White flowers appear in early summer in temperate climates. In cooler areas, chervil will probably only be at its best in the middle of summer. You may even find, in a temperate climate, that chervil will produce growth twice—once in the early spring and then again in early autumn. Nipping off flowering stems will help to encourage lush growth.

Leaves may be harvested at any time. It is better to cut the leaves with scissors rather than pick them, as it is easy to tear the plants accidentally.

CHIVES

Chives, along with green onions (green shallots or scallions) and leeks and garlic, belong to the onion family. Chives are smaller than onions, with narrow spiky tubular leaves growing no more than

30 cm (12 in) high from small round bulbs. In early summer, the round flower heads burst forth in a riot of colour, from purple through to pink, depending on the variety and the soil conditions. They make a very cheerful border plant.

Chives may be propagated by division or from seed. They are obliging herbs, and will grow well under nearly any conditions. Sow six to eight seeds in a flowerpot and then plant out the established clump in midsummer after they have flowered, or in the autumn. Divide the bulbs after the first year, and divide again every three years after that.

Chives are perennial plants and die back completely in the winter, only to send out new growth in the spring. (If this new growth is yellow-green tinged, it means that the soil should be enriched with a good compost). Keep chives well watered, as moisture is essential.

Chives grow well in a pot on the kitchen windowsill, where they are easily reached by the cook, and they look pretty too. They will also do well in larger planter pots, tubs or barrels. If you have planted chives in the garden, weed carefully both beforehand and during the summer (otherwise can be a tricky business differentiating chives from grass).

Most gardening books will advise you to nip off the bright green pompom-like flowers and thus encourage a thicker leaf growth. However, if you don't want to miss out on the eventual bright display, trim them back only after flowering.

Chives do all the better for being continually trimmed: this will result in the plant growing more vigorously and also having a better flavour. When snipping chives, cut several spikes from each of the different plants rather than just lopping one.

In addition to the main variety, common chives or grass onions (*Allium schoenoprasum*), it is also worth growing garlic chives (*A. tuberosum*). Plant them in alternate rows and cut from each while the others are recovering.

CORIANDER

Coriander (also known as Chinese parsley, cilantro and Indian parsley) is a pretty annual with broad, deeply toothed shiny leaves on a slender stem, and grows to a height of 90 cm (36 in).

Set seed in spring directly into moist, moderately rich soil. Like other annuals in the same family, such as dill and parsley, coriander will do best in a fairly light and sunny situation. Sow the seeds thinly and when, after about three weeks, they have germinated, thin the plants as necessary. The seedlings have very long roots and do not transplant well.

Harvest the seedheads at the end of summer when they turn light brown. Allow the seeds to dry in an airy place, and store in airtight jars.

DILL

Dill is a popular and hardy annual, with fine feathery foliage growing from a single stem. It grows to a height of about 90 cm (36 in). Umbels of yellow flowers appear in midsummer, followed by the flat yellow-brown seeds.

Dill has a long tap root, and prefers a soil that is well dug, well drained and moderately deep soil. Sow the seeds in spring directly into their drills in a sunny sheltered spot in the garden. After germination, thin seedlings to about 20 cm (8 in) apart. Water well as the plants are very fast-growing. Try to place plants where they will be protected, either by other plants and herbs, or by a fence or screen, as the stems are spindly and need support.

Dill will self-sow prolifically. Do not plant it near fennel as the two will cross pollinate to produce an odd and useless hybrid. Coriander and chervil are, however, excellent companions for dill.

The flowers, which are very decorative, appear in summer and produce vast amounts of seeds. Harvest them when they begin to turn brown, hanging the flowerheads upside-down in a dry airy space with a sheet underneath to catch the falling seeds.

FENNEL

Fennel is an elegant, tall and hardy plant with large feathery leaves on stiff smooth stems. It bears large umbels of golden flowers in summer followed by a crop of broad brown seeds. The leaves, seeds and bulbous stalk have a strong, sweet aniseed-like taste and smell.

Sow seed in spring in a sunny position and give seedlings plenty of moisture. It is best to plant fennel at the back of the herb garden, for it grows very bushy. Cut the plants back at the end of summer to encourage thick new growth the following spring. Do not water while fennel is dormant, as this can cause root rot.

The leaves can be picked from established plants through till late autumn. The stems may be dried and used to add flavour to winter cookery. Harvest the seed pods in early autumn before they begin to split. Hang them upside down in a warm dry spot over a large sheet to collect the seeds. Dry the seeds in the sun thoroughly before storing them in an airtight jar.

LEMON GRASS

Lemon grass is an evergreen, perennial member of the grass family, and forms large clumps of pale green, aromatic foliage.

It should be grown in a warm, protected position in the garden or in a pot on a sunny balcony. Lemon grass is frost tender, so should be well mulched during the winter months. Keep the water up to it, as it is a 'thirsty herb'.

With its long thin strappy leaves, lemon grass is quite an attractive feature anywhere in the garden, not just in the herb border. A softly waving clump of lemon grass interplanted with a group of scentless flowers, such as irises, can be extremely pretty. Be very careful when you pick the leaves, as they have razor-sharp edges.

LOVAGE

Lovage is a robust, sturdy perennial plant. It has straight hollow stems and broad shiny leaves, and bears umbels of yellow flowers in midsummer. The whole plant has a strong celery-like flavour and fragrance.

Lovage will grow well in most soils, doing best when it is in a rich, moist soil and in partial shade during the day. It can be propagated by seed or by root division but, really, you'll only need one plant in the garden—after three years, it could well have reached a height of 1.8 m (6 ft)! Divide the roots in early spring, making sure that each piece has an 'eye', and plant about 5 cm (2 in) deep into well composted soil.

Water your lovage well during summer and keep it free from weeds. It likes a nice helping of well rotted compost and manure each year, and should be pruned in autumn.

Pick the leaves for immediate use, or dry them on drying racks in a warm airy spot and store in an airtight jar. The seeds may be harvested by clipping the seedheads just before they burst, and then hanging them over a sheet.

MARJORAM

There are many species of marjoram, but the most popular species from a culinary point of view is the sweet-scented *Origanum majorana*.

Marjoram is an easy to grow perennial, growing to about 25 cm (10 in) high. It has pairs of small soft rounded grey–green leaves along fine stems, and pale mauve or white flowers.

Marjoram loves a sunny position and a soil that is light and well drained. In colder climates, sow the fine seeds early in spring under glass, then plant out the seedlings when they're established and any danger of frost has passed. In a warm area, just sow the seed directly into thin drills in the garden bed and thin the plants to about 20 cm (8 in) apart when established. Keep marjoram well weeded: it doesn't like having to compete for space. Cut the plants back after flowering.

To harvest the leaves, pick any time after the flower buds form, but preferably before the buds burst in autumn. Then you should harvest the entire plant, and either dry the branches in loose bunches or strip the leaves and air dry them on a rack in readiness for winter use. Store in an airtight glass jar in a cool dry place.

MINT

There are literally dozens of different kinds of mint, and they all grow very easily. In fact, it's often wise to restrict their enthusiastic root growth by containing the plants, either below ground in a tub or sink, or by planting them in containers.

Mint will grow in almost any soil. Most varieties prefer at least part shade during the day and plenty of water, especially in summer. Some sun is essential in order to produce flavoursome leaves, though quite lush-looking growth will often result in the most shade-bound specimens. In very cold areas you may need to protect the mint roots during the winter with a thick covering of straw.

Encourage bushy growth by pinching back frequently and by cutting back the plants after flowering. In autumn, fork some compost and well rotted manure over your mint. Propagate at this time by root division to encourage vigorous growth. Dig out the entire plant after three or four years, as it will probably have become very woody by then.

For drying, cut the stems just before the flower buds form and place on drying racks or hang in bunches in an airy place. The leaves may be stripped and used whole in cooking, or rubbed through a sieve to form a powder.

NASTURTIUM

The nasturtium (also called Indian cress) has yellow and orange flowers and rounded leaves. Its scent is pleasing, cleanish and peppery. A hardy climbing or trailing annual, nasturtium seeds can be sown in the spring in just about any type of soil, in partial shade or in sun. Nasturtiums tend to become invasive unless trained up wires. They provide a shower of colour during summer. Since snails and slugs love nasturtium foliage of all varieties, you should take appropriate protective measures. Nasturtiums are an excellent garden companion for radishes, cabbages, squash and fruit trees, as they will keep pests at bay.

PARSLEY

Both curly-leafed and flat-leafed parsley are biennial herbs, and easily grown from seed. They reach about 90 cm (36 in) tall by their second year.

Sow the seeds in spring or late summer in a sunny or slightly shaded position, preferably in a well drained and slightly sandy soil. The seeds will take about 8 weeks to germinate. You can decrease this time by soaking the seeds in warm water before you plant them.

Water parsley well in dry weather. Flower stalks, which appear in the second year, should be pinched back to give bushier growth. Parsley will readily self-seed.

The leaves are at their best early on but can be picked and dried in a cool oven until just crisp, then kept in an airtight jar for use year-round. Always pick parsley from the outside, allowing new growth to develop from the middle.

ROSEMARY

There are two main types of this beautiful aromatic evergreen herb, and both have mist-blue flowers: one is a sturdy bush that is suitable for both garden and pot, and the other is a prostrate variety that will cover banks and the tops of sunny brick walls. A row of rosemary bushes makes a fine firm decorative hedge when bushes are grown about 60 cm (24 in) apart and clipped after flowering.

Rosemary will do best in a warm sheltered sunny nook, ideally beside a wall. Soil should be well drained, slightly sandy and on the limey side (the occasional dressing of crushed eggshells will be much appreciated). If your garden soil or aspect is too damp, it is better to grow rosemary in a large terracotta pot indoors on a sunny windowsill. Always 'crock' the base of a pot with broken pottery shards to facilitate drainage—rosemary hates to have wet feet.

Rosemary can be started from seed but cuttings take very easily and this is usually the preferred method. Take cuttings with a 'heel', dip them in a starter mix, and set in a well drained sandy potting mix. If you life in a frost-prone area, keep the new rosemary plants indoors or under glass for the first winter. Clip rosemary every autumn and pinch out new growth in the spring to encourage bushiness.

SAGE

Sage is a shrubby woody plant. The main variety, *Salvia officinalis*, has grey–green leaves, but some varieties offer highly decorative variegated leaves, notably the red or purple sage, *S. officinalis purpurea*. The delicious pineapple-flavoured form, *S. rutans*, is also becoming better known. Sage flowers are generally purple or blue with a lighter scent and flavour than that of the leaves.

Sage grows well in most types of soil. Seeds may be sown in spring but, as they do not always breed true, it is best to take cuttings from established plants. Plant out the cuttings in a warm dry spot where the sun will catch them, and put a little compost around them—they strike quite easily, so little other preparation is needed.

When it has finished blooming, trim back the bush and it will grow into a compact bush about a metre (36 in) high. After about four years it may straggle unattractively and become too woody, but new plants can be grown from its cutting.

Prune mature bushes hard in autumn to ensure vigorous growth to harvest. Clip stems before flower buds open, cutting back to about 15 cm (6 in) above the ground. Strip the leaves, dry them, and store in an airtight container. Discard the stems, as they have too strong and acrid a flavour.

SALAD BURNET

Salad burnet is a hardy perennial. It is a pretty and graceful herb with dainty leaflets and rosette-like flowers, and is often the first plant to appear in spring and the last to die back in the autumn.

Although a perennial, salad burnet self-sows like an annual. You can leave the seeds to sprout where they fall, or you can collect them by placing bags over the ripe flower heads. Sow seeds in autumn, in shallow drills 30 cm (12 in) or so apart. You can also propagate salad burnet by dividing the roots in spring or autumn.

Salad burnet thrives on neglect, preferring a very poor and chalky soil. It does, however, need to be kept free from weeds and watered well during a dry summer.

Trim the stems back when they are about 10 cm (4 in) long: only the young leaves and tops should be picked for culinary use. Also, if you are growing salad burnet exclusively as a kitchen herb, you must pick off the flower stems as soon as they appear, otherwise its flavour becomes tough and bitter.

SAVORY

There are two main types of these aromatic plants: summer savory (*Satureja hortensis*) and winter savory (*S. montant*). The summer savory is more popular for culinary use, being sweeter.

Summery savory is an annual, and grows to about 45 cm (18 in) high. It has narrow leaves and small white, mauve or pink flowers on purplish stems. It is easy to grow from seeds or cuttings. Sow seeds in a well drained soil and compost lightly. Germination is slow. The preferred position for summer savory is in full sun and they should be watered frequently; thin seedlings to about 30 cm (12 in) apart.

Summer savory dries quickly and stores well. Harvest the leaves when the plants are about 15 cm (6 in) high, and cut them back after flowering.

Winter savory is a perennial, woody plant that grows to about 30 cm (12 in) high. It is particularly suitable for growing as a low clipped hedge in the garden, as it has a very compact growth habit. Its leaves are similar to summer savory, but a darker green and with sharper tips.

In spring, propagation of winter savory is commonly by way of cuttings of the young shoots, taken with a 'heel' attached; in autumn, by root division. It is, however, easily grown from seed. Winter savory will prefer a poorer soil than summer savory, but shares its summer cousin's liking for full sun.

SORREL

Sorrel is a perennial with broad flat leaves resembling spearheads and spikes of reddish–brown flowers which appear from early summer onwards. It grows to a height of 90 cm (36 in).

There are two main types of sorrel which are good as 'pot herbs': garden sorrel (*Rumex acetosa*) and French sorrel (*R. scutatus*). The latter is considered the most tasty and succulent but is not necessarily as readily available as garden sorrel.

Sorrel can be propagated from seed or by way of root division. Sorrel will obligingly grow in most soils, but prefers a moist rich bed to which a generous helping of well rotted compost has been added. If using seed, sow in early spring in a spot which catches sun or partial shade. Thin the seedlings to 20 cm (8 in) apart when they are about the height of your little finger.

Be sure to cut down the flowering stems, to give a bushy plant with a good crop of leaves. The leaves may be dried and stored but this is not really necessary as a good clump should carry right through all but the most bitter winter. Use the new fresh leaves for stronger seasoning of stews and soups in winter. A sorrel plant will last for years, but should be divided every three or four years to stop the roots becoming too tightly bound.

TARRAGON

French (or 'true') tarragon (*Artemisia dracunculus*) is considered infinitely superior to the Russian (or 'false') tarragon (*A. dracunculoides*) in both flavour and scent. French tarragon is a much smaller plant than the Russian, growing only to about 90 cm (36 in) tall, and has narrow, dark green, shiny leaves and tiny greenish flowers.

Tarragon may be propagated by way of cuttings or root division. It is quite difficult to grow from seed. Both the tarragons like a sunny aspect and, true to their Mediterranean and Asian origin, prefer a poor dry soil. A too-wet or too-rich soil will affect the characteristic flavour and 'bite'.

Tarragon roots spread rapidly by means of runners so, unless you want a

very large patch of tarragon, you will need to lift, divide and replant the roots every year or so. This will produce bushier plants and better-flavoured leaves. Cut tarragon plants right back each autumn and cover the roots with straw if your area is prone to frost.

One odd old piece of advice says that, in order to ensure a good growth of tarragon, you should pull up the plant when it is about 30 cm (12 in) high—only to reset it immediately in the same hole!

THYME

There are a very great many different varieties of thyme. Apart from common thyme (*Thymus vulgaris*), there is a prostrate creeping thyme (*T. serpyllum*), caraway-scented thyme (*T. herbabarona*), and lemon thyme (*T. x citriodorus*). All share similar properties, being highly aromatic and sturdy plants that do well in poor soil with a warm dry aspect.

Thyme is a perennial, many-branched, woody shrub; it reaches a height of about 30 cm (12 in). Common thyme, which is the one most used in cookery, has small paired grey–green leaves and tiny whitish or mauve flowers that appear in midsummer. It grows best in a sandy well drained soil to which some lime or mortar crumblings have been added. It will produce a far more powerful flavour in a warm dry spot than in a damp one.

Propagate thyme from seeds, cuttings or root division. The seeds should be sown in spring but they need a warm soil to germinate so, if you live in a colder climate, you'd best start them off in a pot indoors. Take cuttings in summer, with a 'heel' attached, dust with starter powder, and plant them in a seedling box filled with a mixture of wet sand and good quality potting mix.

All the thymes are said to do well near other herbs of Mediterranean origin, notably lavender and rosemary, and are much loved by bees.

WATERCRESS

Watercress's name is a direct reference to its preferred growth habit—it does best in fresh running water, especially where the soil nearby has a high lime content.

Don't pick wild watercress, as the stream or creek may be polluted, and only an expert can really tell the difference between watercress and the similar (but poisonous) umbelliferous plant known as 'fool's cress'.

Watercress is a perennial, and lives for many years. It will grow to 45 cm (18 in) high, and bears rather uninteresting smallish white flowers in summer. The leaves are bright green and have a characteristic hot and tangy taste.

Watercress may be grown from seed or root cuttings submerged in mud or, ideally, shallow water in a semi shaded position. If you have access to the damp bank of a stream, you could try your luck there. Otherwise it is possible to grow it as part of a backyard watergarden, utilising old laundry tubs, for instance. Remember that the water needs to be changed regularly as the watercress will go rotten in stagnant water.

Once established, watercress will spread rapidly by way of root division. The more you trim it back, the bushier and quicker it will grow, giving a rich supply of leaves for use in summer salads, soups and sauces.

VIETNAMESE MINT

Despite its name, this is not really a member of the mint family. It is a fast growing perennial with spikes of small pink flowers in summer. It reaches approximately 80 cm (32 in) high. It is easily struck from cuttings set out in a moist sunny position in a rich well-composted soil. In fact, as is the case with so many herbs, the problem is more likely to be how to hold it back, as it rapidly becomes invasive in a garden.

GLOSSARY OF TERMS

AUSTRALIAN	*UK*	*USA*
EQUIPMENT AND TERMS		
aluminium foil	cooking foil	aluminum foil
can	tin	can
frying pan	frying pan	skillet
griller	grill	broiler
greaseproof paper	greaseproof paper	waxproof paper
paper towel	kitchen paper	white paper towel
plastic wrap	cling film	plastic wrap
seeded	stoned	pitted
INGREDIENTS		
artichoke	globe artichoke	artichoke
bacon rasher	bacon rasher	bacon slice
black olive	black olive	ripe olive
broad bean	broad bean	fava bean
butternut pumpkin		butternut squash
capsicum	pepper	sweet pepper
chicken breast fillets	chicken breast fillets	boneless chicken breasts
chickpea	chickpea	garbanzo bean
chilli	chilli	chili
coriander (fresh)	coriander/Indian parsley	cilantro/Chinese parsley
corn kernels	sweet corn	corn kernels
cornflour	cornflour	cornstarch
cornmeal	polenta/maize meal	cornmeal
cream	single cream	light cream
desiccated coconut	desiccated coconut	shredded coconut
dill	dill	dill weed
eggplant	aubergine	eggplant
gelatine	gelatine powder	gelatin
pawpaw	pawpaw	papaya or papaw
pine nut	pine nut	pignolias
plain flour	(general purpose) flour	all-purpose flour
prawn	prawn or shrimp	shrimp
silver beet (spinach)	silver beet (chard)	Swiss chard
snow pea	mangetout, sugar pea	snow pea
soybean	soyabean	soybean
sultanas	sultanas	seedless white or golden raisins
thickened cream	double cream	heavy or whipping cream
tomato paste	tomato purée	tomato paste
Worcestershire sauce	Worcester sauce	Worchestershire sauce
yoghurt	natural yogurt	unflavoured yoghurt
zucchini	courgette	zucchini

MEASURING MADE EASY

How to Measure Liquids

METRIC	IMPERIAL	CUPS
30 ml	1 fl oz	1 tablespoon plus 2 teaspoons
60 ml	2 fl oz	¼ cup
90 ml	3 fl oz	
125 ml	4 fl oz	½ cup
150 ml	5 fl oz	
170 ml	5½ fl oz	
180 ml	6 fl oz	¾ cup
220 ml	7 fl oz	
250 ml	8 fl oz	1 cup
500 ml	16 fl oz	2 cups
600 ml	20 fl oz (1 pint)	2½ cups

How to Measure Dry Ingredients

15 g	½ oz	
30 g	1 oz	
60 g	2 oz	
90 g	3 oz	
125 g	4 oz	(¼ lb)
155 g	5 oz	
185 g	6 oz	
220 g	7 oz	
250 g	8 oz	(½ lb)
280 g	9 oz	
315 g	10 oz	
345 g	11 oz	
375 g	12 oz	(¾ lb)
410 g	13 oz	
440 g	14 oz	
470 g	15 oz	
500 g	16 oz	(1 lb)
750 g	24 oz	(1½ lb)
1 kg	32 oz	(2 lb)

Quick Conversions

5 mm	¼ in	
1 cm	½ in	
2 cm	¾ in	
2.5 cm	1 in	
5 cm	2 in	
6 cm	2½ in	
8 cm	3 in	
10 cm	4 in	
12 cm	5 in	
15 cm	6 in	
18 cm	7 in	
20 cm	8 in	
23 cm	9 in	
25 cm	10 in	
28 cm	11 in	
30 cm	12 in	(1 ft)
46 cm	18 in	
50 cm	20 in	
61 cm	24 in	(2 ft)

NOTE:

We developed the recipes in this book in Australia where the tablespoon measure is 20 ml. In many other countries the tablespoon is 15 ml. For most recipes this difference will not be noticeable. However, for recipes using baking powder, gelatine, bicarbonate of soda, small amounts of flour and cornflour, we suggest you add an extra teaspoon for each tablespoon specified.

Using Cups and Spoons

All cup and spoon measurements are level

METRIC CUP

¼ cup	60 ml	2 fl oz
⅓ cup	80 ml	2½ fl oz
½ cup	125 ml	4 fl oz
1 cup	250 ml	8 fl oz

METRIC SPOONS

¼ teaspoon	1.25 ml
½ teaspoon	2.5 ml
1 teaspoon	5 ml
1 tablespoon	20 ml

Oven Temperatures

TEMPERATURES	CELSIUS (°C)	FAHRENHEIT (°F)	GAS MARK
Very slow	120	250	½
Slow	150	300	2
Moderately slow	160-180	325-350	3-4
Moderate	190-200	375-400	5-6
Moderately hot	220-230	425-450	7
Hot	250-260	475-500	8-9

INDEX TO RECIPES

STOCKISTS

Accoutrement
611 Military Road, Mosman NSW
Tel. (02) 969 1031

The Bay Tree
40 Holdsworth Street, Woollahra NSW
Tel. (02) 328 1101

Gempo
100 Harris Street, Pyrmont NSW
Tel. (02) 552 1199

Hale Imports
97-99 Old Pittwater Road, Brookvale NSW
Tel. (02) 938 2400

Innerspace
100 Harris Street, Pyrmont NSW
Tel. (02) 692 0344

Les Olivades
2 Transvaal Avenue, Double Bay NSW
Tel. (02) 327 8073

Milkwood
147 William Street, East Sydney NSW
Tel. (02) 360 5852

J.D. Milner & Assoc.
100 Harris Street, Pyrmont NSW
Tel. (02) 660 4033

Plumes Gift Agencies
100 Harris Street, Pyrmont NSW
Tel. (02) 552 3939

Potter Williams
100 Harris Street, Pyrmont NSW
Tel. (02) 552 2233

South Pacific Fabrics
15-19 Boundary Street, Rushcutters Bay NSW
Tel. (02) 360 1199

Studio Haus
10 Transvaal Avenue, Double Bay NSW
Tel. (02) 326 2044

Swing Gifts
100 Harris Street, Pyrmont NSW
Tel. (02) 566 4419

Whitehouse Interior Design
74 Queen Street, Woollahra NSW
Tel. (02) 328 7894

HERBS

All herbs supplied and air-freighted to Sydney from Melbourne by Australian Herb Supplies
662 Smith Street, Clifton Hill, Vic 3068
P.O. Box 28, Clifton Hill 3068
Tel. (03) 482 3188; toll free 008 805 392
Fax (03) 482 2282
Distribution centres:
Melbourne: Tel. (03) 482 3188
Sydney: Tel. 018 566 382
Brisbane: Tel. 018 789 615;
Fax/Tel. (075) 45 1713

ACKNOWLEDGMENTS

Some of the recipes in this book were published previously in: Mary-Lou Arnold (comp.), *Good Health Cookbook: Wholefood Recipes for All the Family*, Bay Books, 1985; Doug Marsland (contrib.), *Indian Cooking*, Bay Books, 1979; *Indian Cookery*, Bay Books, 1992; Frances Hutchinson (ed.), *The Easy Cookbook for a Busy Lifestyle*, Bay Books, 1984; Janice Baker, *Herbs for Better Living*, Bay Books, 1992.

A Bay Books Publication
Bay Books, an imprint of
HarperCollins*Publishers*
25 Ryde Road, Pymble, Sydney NSW 2073, Australia
31 View Road, Glenfield, Auckland 10, New Zealand

First published in Australia in 1994

National Library of Australia
Cataloguing-in-Publication data:

Francis, Kay, 1952- .
  A handful of herbs.
  Includes index.
  ISBN 1 86378 146 3.
  1.Cookery (herbs). 2.Herbs. I.Allardice, Pamela, 1958- .
  II.Title.
641.657

Photography: Rowan Fotheringham
Food stylist: Kay Francis
Food stylist's assistant: Dominique Marill
Front cover recipe: Harlequin Pizza, page 39 (Christopher Vine platter from Plumes Gift Agencies. Chair from Innerspace. Blue stripe fabric, Etamine 'Thalie' from South Pacific Fabrics. Green stripe background fabric, table napkins and placemat from Whitehouse Interior Design.)
Printed by Griffin Press, Adelaide
Printed in Australia

9 8 7 6 5 4 3 2 1
97 96 95 94